DISCARD
Centerville Library
Washington-Centerville Public Library
Centerville, Ohio

W9-BBH-721

MAKERY

For Millie

Makery
by Kate Smith

First published in Great Britain in 2013
by Mitchell Beazley, an imprint of
Octopus Publishing Group Ltd,
Endeavour House,
189 Shaftesbury Avenue,
London, WC2H 8JY
www.octopusbooks.co.uk

An Hachette UK Company
www.hachette.co.uk

Copyright © Octopus Publishing Group Ltd 2013
Text copyright © Kate Smith 2013

Specially commissioned photography
by Aliki Kirmitsi & Ania Wawrzkowicz
and Marc Wilson

All rights reserved. No part of this work may be
reproduced or utilised in any form or by any means,
electronic or mechanical, including photocopying,
recording or by any information storage and
retrieval system, without the prior written
permission of the publishers.

ISBN 9781845337049

A CIP record for this book is available from the
British Library

Set in Pluto and Julieta Pro

Printed and bound in China

Created by Harris + Wilson

Design: A-Side Studio
Managing editor: Caroline Harris
Text editor: Judy Barratt
Illustrations: Martha Gavin
Assistant Production Manager: Lucy Carter

The use of super glue, hammers, nails and other
materials and tools as recommended in this book
should be done with care and in accordance with
the manufacturers' instructions. Although all
reasonable care has been taken in the preparation
of this book, neither the author nor the publisher
can accept any liability for any consequences
arising from the use of the book, or the information
contained within.

MAKERY

OVER 30 PROJECTS FOR THE HOME, TO WEAR AND TO GIVE

KATE SMITH

MITCHELL
BEAZLEY

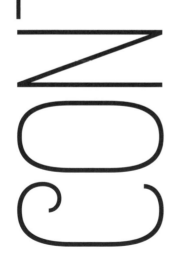

CONTENTS

INTRODUCTION

⨯⨯⨯

It took me a while to realise that 'Making' was what I should do as a career, but looking back it was actually quite obvious: I've made things for as long as I can remember and have always taken great pleasure in it. My first commercial craft venture was at the age of eight, when a friend and I set up a stall called Bobtail Crafts at the local church fete to sell our handmade Fimo creations. We mightn't have made much financially, but it was great fun. We took it ever so seriously, even designing our own logo and business cards.

I sewed my way through university, supplementing my income by tailoring end-of-term ball dresses for friends and stitching repairs for the sports clubs. Then through my 12 years working in London's media industry, I satisfied my creative urges by making bags for my Portobello Road stall, and running up friends' wedding dresses.

My first love is sewing; I can spend hours poring over fabrics, and turning them into clothes, gifts or homewares. But like many other crafty types, I can turn my hand to most creative techniques, and I soon learned the pleasure to be had from sharing these skills with others. My husband and I started The Makery in 2009; it's a craft workshop space in Bath – and now a shop, too, selling all the 'ingredients' to make beautiful projects. In the beginning we ran workshops and parties in sewing, knitting, crochet and upholstery. Now we include lampshade-making, purse-making, printmaking – the list grows as our audience tells us what they are hungry to know. We have won an award for our creativity and innovation, and run countless workshops with schools and charities.

My aim is for contemporary craft to be accessible to everyone. Nothing delights me more than seeing a group of guests arrive at The Makery, unsure of their creative ability yet enthusiastic to learn. They gradually grasp the skills, and inevitably finish with an immense sense of pride and confidence, keen to further their newfound knowledge and spend more time making. It's powerful stuff!

I also happen to think it's incredibly important that we don't lose all these wonderful artisan skills and techniques. I'm not saying everyone should make their own clothes and darn their socks, but it's important that we all understand how things are made, and can sew on a button at the very least.

With this book, I've brought together some of my favourite projects, and ones that our visitors have asked how to make. It is arranged in three sections – so you can choose whether to make something to wear, something for your home, or a special gift. At the back there's a section on crafting basics, with my tips for getting a professional result. On each project I've given an idea of the level of difficulty and how long it is likely to take. Many people can be heard to say they 'don't have a creative bone in their body', but I reckon that if you break down the techniques, use familiar language and make the projects relevant, even the most reluctant crafter can make something to be proud of.

'Makery' is a lot like cookery – if you start with gorgeous, high-quality ingredients, you're well on the way to creating something beautiful. Leaf through the pages of this book to find inspiration for your own fabric, button and yarn choices.

There really is nothing quite like the sense of pride to be had from creating something yourself out of a few pieces of fabric and other bits and bobs. Our vision for The Makery of teaching as many people as possible to get into the crafty spirit is certainly happening, and I couldn't be happier. I hope you enjoy the projects in this book, and feel inspired to make more!

Kate Smith
The Makery, Bath

Decoupage Pendant

TIME

THIS PROJECT ISN'T TOO FIDDLY, SO SHOULD TAKE NO MORE THAN AN HOUR OR TWO.

I've got a thing about framed insects – beautiful butterflies and beetles, especially. They were my inspiration for this pretty pendant, although I can guarantee no animals were harmed in the making! Make sure you gather all the materials before you get started. It may seem like a big outlay when you first buy them – but don't worry, everything you buy, you'll use time and again.

MATERIALS

METAL PENDANT BASE (SEE PAGE 155 FOR STOCKISTS)

SCRAP PAPER TO MAKE THE TEMPLATE

PRETTY PAPER FOR THE MOTIF, SUCH AS A WALLPAPER SAMPLE

SPRAY FIXATIVE (SEE PAGE 155 FOR STOCKISTS)

GLUE (GLOSS OR MATT MOD PODGE WORKS BEST; SEE PAGE 155 FOR STOCKISTS)

MOD PODGE DIMENSIONAL MAGIC (SEE PAGE 155 FOR STOCKISTS)

TOOLS

PAPER SCISSORS

PENCIL

ERASER

PREPARE THE PENDANT MOTIF

1. First, make a template for your pendant.
   The best way to do this is to take the pendant
   base, and press it face down firmly onto a piece
   of scrap paper. It should leave an indented line
   the shape of the pendant aperture. (See Figure 1.)
   Carefully cut this out, cutting inside the shape so
   that you create a window the shape and size of
   the pendant aperture.

2. Next, choose the area of your motif paper you
   would like to feature in the pendant. You can
   hold your template window over the paper to
   check for size and position. When you're happy,
   lightly draw a pencil line inside the template
   onto your paper, and carefully cut it out – erring
   on the outside of your pencil line. Gently rub out
   the pencil line if it's still visible after you've done
   the cutting.

3. Lightly spray the paper image with fixative
   (this will ensure the ink doesn't run) and allow
   the fixative to dry.

MAKE THE RESIN PENDANT

1. Apply a thin layer of glue inside the pendant
   base, and stick the image in place. Allow the
   glue to dry.

2. Now the fun bit! Apply lots of Mod Podge
   Dimensional Magic on top of your paper image.
   If the pendant doesn't have a raised edge,
   apply a line around the edge first, then fill in
   the centre. If you do have a raised edge, you can
   load up inside it with the Magic to give a slightly
   domed effect. The product will appear cloudy at
   first, but it will set clear so that it appears that
   your image is set in resin.

3. Allow the Mod Podge Dimensional Magic to
   dry completely (it will take about three hours)
   before using your pendant.

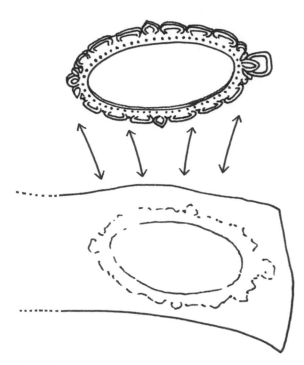

Figure 1

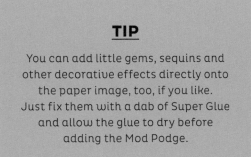

TIP

You can add little gems, sequins and
other decorative effects directly onto
the paper image, too, if you like.
Just fix them with a dab of Super Glue
and allow the glue to dry before
adding the Mod Podge.

CLASP PURSE

These clasps make gorgeous purses and bags. The type of fabric you choose really changes the style. I've gone for some linen, trimmed with beautiful, handmade Victorian lace for a delicate look. Coarser fabrics such as cotton and linen are also easier to work with while you're getting used to these clasps. When you're more confident, a purse made from silk would look amazing.

TIME

MAKING THESE CLASP PURSES IS QUITE FIDDLY, SO YOU NEED SOME TIME AND PATIENCE. ALLOW A COUPLE OF SITTINGS FOR YOUR FIRST ATTEMPT.

MATERIALS

MEDIUM IRON-ON INTERFACING: 50CM X 25CM (20IN X 10IN)

OUTER FABRIC: 50CM X 25CM (20IN X 10IN)

LINING FABRIC: 50CM X 25CM (20IN X 10IN)

CLASP: 17CM (6¾IN) AT ITS WIDEST POINT IN THIS CASE, BUT YOU CAN ADAPT THE PATTERN TO FIT ANY SIZE

PAPER TWINE: 2 X 30CM (12IN) LENGTHS

TOOLS

IRON

PATTERN PROVIDED AT THE BACK OF THIS BOOK

FABRIC SCISSORS

PINS

NEEDLE AND THREAD

SEWING MACHINE

GLUE (WE RECOMMEND GÜTERMANN HT2 FABRIC GLUE)

COCKTAIL STICKS

PLIERS (JEWELLERY PLIERS OR DIY TOOLBOX PLIERS WILL DO)

SCRAP OF FABRIC OR FELT TO PROTECT THE CLASP

PREPARE THE PURSE PIECES

1. Iron the interfacing onto the wrong side of your outer fabric to strengthen it, following the instructions on the pack.

2. Use the pattern to cut out 2 x clasp purse pieces from the lining fabric and 2 x clasp purse pieces from the outer fabric, ensuring you match the grain on all the pieces by aligning it with the arrow on the pattern. Snip the notches, and mark points A, B and C with pins.

3. Now you're ready to sew. First you need to make pleats in all the purse pieces to give your clasp purse a lovely 'puffy' shape that will also optimise the space inside. To do this, take one of your pieces of fabric and fold it in half, right sides facing, matching up the notches at the top.

4. Pin vertically at the notch, then line up the halfway fold with the pin and open out the fabric to either side to make a pleat with two vertical folds. Iron flat (see Figure 1).

5. Tack the pleat in place, close to the raw outer edge (see Figure 1). Repeat this step for the other three pieces. You can vary the look of your purse by the way you fold your fabric in half – with the pleat on the outside or the inside; experiment before you sew to see which you prefer.

SEW UP THE PURSE

1. Pin the two lining pieces together with right sides facing. Machine stitch around the bottom curved edge, from point A to point B, with a 1cm (¼in) seam allowance. Make sure you secure your stitching at the start and end by reversing. Carefully clip the curves to give a neater finish. (See Figure 2, over the page.) Repeat with the outer fabric pieces, and open out the seams at the sides so that they lie flat.

2. The following steps can get a bit fiddly. You should now have two pouches: one lining and one outer. Turn the lining pouch right side out and sit it inside your outer pouch, matching the side seams. The right sides of the lining and outer should be facing. Pin the pouches together at the side seams.

3. Place the purse in front of you, so that one of the side seams is facing you. By hand (which is easier at this point), use backstitch to stitch from point C on one side of the seam to point C on the other side (see page 148; your stitches will form a smile shape). Sew through both fabrics, leaving a 1cm (¼in) seam allowance.

4. Clip the curve a couple of times with your scissors, taking care not to cut your stitches. Turn the pouch around and repeat for the other side seam.

5. Now turn the outer fabric pouch right side out, and manoeuvre the lining pouch so that it sits inside the outer. You'll probably think you've made a mistake at this point and it will all seem a bit wonky, but it should look right soon enough. Concentrate on one element at a time: outer, then lining. You will end up with a nice neat, lined purse pouch when the pieces are correctly turned out.

6. Match the top (raw) edges of fabric, lining to outer, on each side of the purse. Sew about 10cm (4in) of running stitch by hand along the top curve, close to the edge. This is just to hold the pieces together while you fix the clasp.

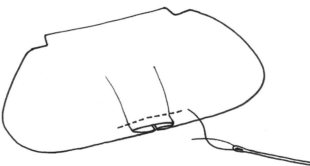

Figure 1

ATTACH THE CLASP

1. OK, here we go... the nitty gritty. With the clasp fully open, drop some glue into the channel on one side. Not too thick – you don't want it to ooze out on to your fabric.

2. Take your pouch and match the centre point of one side of the pouch with the centre point of the glued side of the clasp (find the centre point by folding the pouch in half, matching the side seams). Make sure you have the clasp the right way round, so that its outside matches with the fabric outer of the purse.

3. Insert the fabric into the frame, nudging it in with a cocktail stick so that it is tucked right into the clasp channel (see Figure 3). When you're happy with the positioning, quickly push a length of the paper twine in between the fabric and clasp (on the interior side), to hold it in place and fill the gap between the fabric and clasp. You might find that when you push one side in, the other side comes out a bit. Stay with it!

4. With the first side of your purse fully inserted into the clasp, take your pliers and gently squeeze down on the clasp at either end. I like to pop a scrap of fabric or felt between the pliers and clasp so that the pliers don't leave scratches. Then gently squeeze down all the way around the frame to secure the fabric in place.

5. You'll notice that the twine extends beyond the end of the clasp – don't worry, just trim it off so that you can't see it.

6. Repeat these steps with the other side of the fabric pouch. You should find it slightly easier this time, as the fabric is already more or less held in place on the first side.

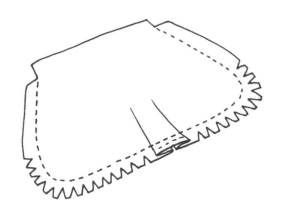

Figure 2

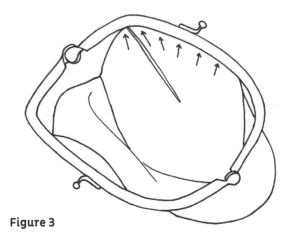

Figure 3

TIPS

You can buy all sorts of styles and sizes of clasp, either sew-in, or glue-in, as in this project. I would say the sew-in kind are slightly easier to use, but I prefer the glue-in look. Clasp stockists are listed on page 155.

If you can't source twisted paper string, the string sometimes used for the handles of brown-paper bags works perfectly instead.

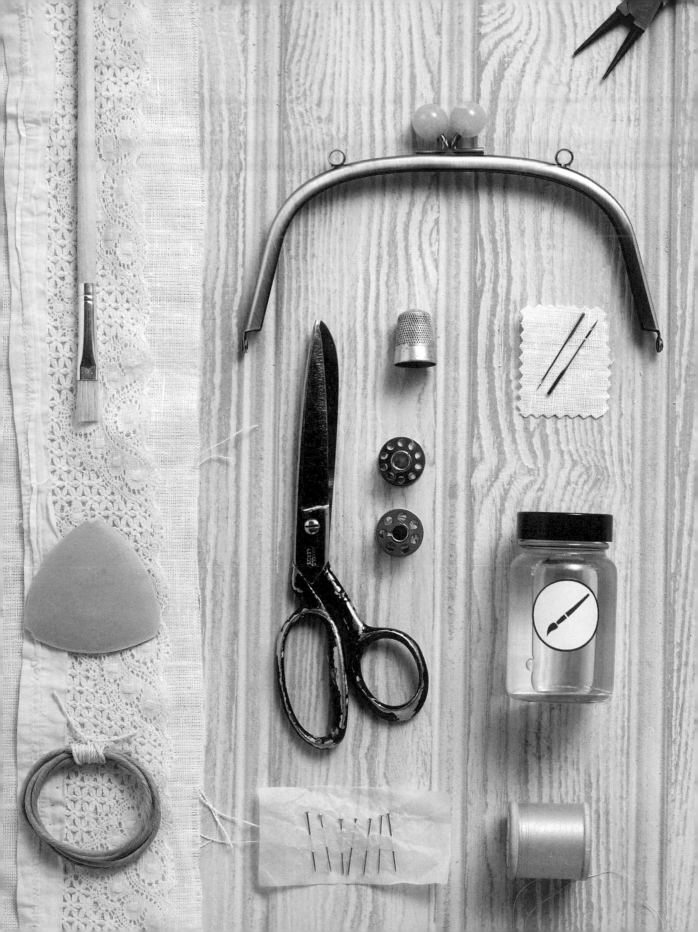

CROCHET SLIPPERS

TIME

IF YOU'RE A BEGINNER THIS MIGHT TAKE A GOOD FEW EVENINGS. OR IF YOU'RE QUICK, YOU COULD MAKE ONE SLIPPER A NIGHT AND DO IT IN TWO.

Now, I'm no crocheter, but I knew exactly what I wanted for this project. For expertise, I called upon The Makery's formidable crochet teacher, Sara Huntington, and she whipped up this pattern, just like that. We've tried the results on lots of our friends, and the slippers seem to magically fit anyone from a UK size 3 to 7 (US 5½ to 9½). They are honestly the most comfortable slippers I've ever worn, and the cherries set them off a treat! For the basics of crochet and understanding all the ch and dc see page 153.

MATERIALS

1 X SKEIN DEBBIE BLISS DONEGAL LUXURY TWEED, CHUNKY (WE USED COLOUR 33502)

1 X EMBELLISHMENT (WE USED CROCHETED CHERRIES)

CO-ORDINATING POLYESTER THREAD

TOOLS

6MM (¼IN) CROCHET HOOK

A STITCH MARKER, SUCH AS A LARGE SAFETY PIN

DARNING NEEDLE

EMBROIDERY SCISSORS

NEEDLE

MAKE THE SLIPPERS

1. Chain (ch) 4 and join the last chain with a slip stitch into the first chain to form a circle (see Figure 1). Try not to pull the yarn too taut, or the slippers won't stretch.

2. Make two chain stitches at the beginning of your first row (to bring the hook up to height). Then work in a spiral formation, making double chain stitches (dc) around the ring, by inserting the hook into the central space each time (not the chain stitches from your first ring). Row 1: 8 dc into centre of circle (8 dc).

3. When you get back to where you started on the ring, you need to join your stitches to complete the ring. To do this, insert the needle into the first stitch on the ring and create a slip stitch (see Figure 2).

4. Place your safety pin or other marker into the last dc (you will move it to the last stitch of each of the following rounds to help you keep track). Continue in a spiral formation, but now you will be inserting the needle into the stitches of the previous row, not the central circle.

   Row 2: (1 dc into first dc, 2dc into next dc) four times (12 dc).

   Row 3: (1 dc into first and second dc, 2dc in next dc) four times (16 dc).

   Row 4: (1 dc into first, second and third dc, 2dc in next dc) four times (20 dc).

   Rows 5–12: 1 dc into each dc (20 dc).

   Row 13: 1 ch, 1 dc into each of the next 16 dc (16 dc).

5. Place another marker on the last stitch and turn. Working on these 16 dc stitches between the markers only, continue as follows:

   Rows 14–22: 1 ch, 1 dc into each dc.

   Row 23: (increase row) 1 ch, 2 dc into first dc, 1 DC into next 14 dc, 2 dc into last dc (18 dc).

   Rows 24–25: 1 ch, 1 dc into each DC (18 dc).

   Row 26: (increase row) 1 ch, 2 dc into first dc, 1 dc into next 16 dc, 2 dc into last dc (20 dc).

   Rows 27–28: 1 ch, 1 dc into each dc.

6. Fasten off, leaving a long tail for sewing up.

7. Use the darning needle to sew up the slipper. Bring the side sections of the heel end of the slipper together and invert them, so they are inside out. Sew the edges together (see page 154) from top to bottom to make the inside back heel seam of the slipper.

8. Repeat steps 1 to 6 to make your second slipper.

9. With the needle and thread, stitch the embellishment on to one slipper in your desired position.

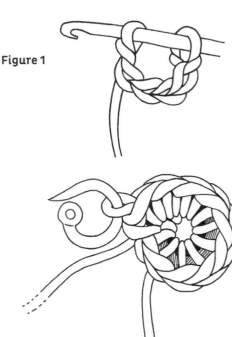

Figure 1

Figure 2

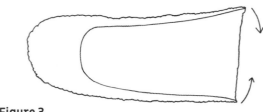

Figure 3

TIP

These slippers are very stretchy, but if you like you can adapt them by increasing or decreasing the width of the toe and adding or removing spiral increase rows. You can alter the length of the slipper by increasing or decreasing the number of rows between 16 and 22 in the pattern.

WRIST WARMERS

TIME

THESE SHOULD BE DOABLE IN A WEEK'S-WORTH OF EVENINGS

The lovely and very talented Jessica of Yiskah Knits (www.yiskahknits.co.uk) designed these beauties. I love that they'll keep you nice and warm, yet won't hamper your ability to use your hands! If you're a knitting beginner, see the guide to starting and stitches on page 152.

MATERIALS

1 X SKEIN DEBBIE BLISS DONEGAL LUXURY TWEED, CHUNKY

BUTTONS AND LACE FOR DECORATION (WE USED WOODEN BUTTONS AND CROCHETED LACE)

CO-ORDINATING POLYESTER THREAD

TOOLS

PAIR 6MM (¼IN) KNITTING NEEDLES

DARNING NEEDLE

EMBROIDERY SCISSORS

NEEDLE

KNIT THE SLEEVES

1. Cast on 24 stitches, then start knitting the first two rows. Row 1: knit (K) all stitches. Row 2: purl (P) all stitches.

2. Repeat these two rows a further 13 times, so you end up with 28 rows, or until your work measures 16cm (6in) in length. Be sure to end on a purl (wrong-side) row.

MAKE THE THUMBHOLE

1. This is made over the next two rows. You'll notice from the instructions below that these two rows are slightly different, depending on which hand you're knitting for – this is to ensure the seam sits comfortably in the same place on each hand. The right hand is given in brackets – so, Left Hand (Right Hand).

   Row 29: K7 (K13), cast off 4 stitches, K12 (K6).

   Remember you will need to knit two additional stitches to begin the cast-off. Once you have finished casting off the four stitches, you'll be left with one stitch on your right needle and can proceed to knit the remaining 12 (six) on the left.

2. Row 30: P13 (P7), turn your work, cast on four stitches, turn your work, P7 (P13).

   When you reach the gap created by the cast-off stitches, turn your work and you will see the knit (right-side) rows facing you. The working yarn will be on your left needle.

   Now cast on four stitches: to do this, insert your right needle into the first stitch, wrap the stitch as if to knit and pull through, but then rather than removing the stitch from the needle, twist it and place the loop back on the left needle.

   Once you have four new stitches, turn your work back around so the wrong side is facing you, and purl across the remaining seven (13) stitches. You'll need to pull the first purl stitch tighter than usual to avoid creating a hole next to your thumbhole.

KNIT THE HAND

1. Row 31: K all stitches. The new cast-on stitches may be tight at first, so take your time on this row.

2. Row 32: P all stitches. You should now be able to see your thumbhole appearing!

3. Continue working alternate K and P rows for another 10 rows, or until your work measures 5cm (2in) from your thumbhole.

4. Last row: cast off all stitches.

FINISH YOUR WRIST WARMERS

1. Sew up the seam to bring your wrist warmers to life. To do this, cut a 38cm to 50cm (15in to 20in) length of yarn and thread it onto your darning needle. Fold the two sides of your wrist warmer together and thread the yarn through the very bottom left corner of your piece. Move across and pass your needle through the opposite bottom right corner to anchor the sides together.

2. Find the first vertical column of V-shaped stitches on each side. Pull the Vs apart gently so that you can see a series of bars between the stitches, like a ladder.

3. Thread your needle under the first two bars on the left-hand side, and then across and under the first two bars on the right-hand side. Continue up the rest of the seam in this way, in a zigzag pattern. Every 2cm to 3cm (1in) or so, pull the yarn tight to zip the seam closed. That's my favourite bit!

4. You'll see that the seam is almost completely unnoticeable. Now just weave in all your ends securely, and you're ready to personalise your wrist warmers. Sew on lace, buttons, or your choice of decoration.

TIP

It's a good idea to go slow with the thumbhole, and pull the purl stitches either side of it tighter than normal by pulling down on the working yarn. There may still be a slight gap, but this will minimise it a lot! It's the same with the seaming at the end – you want to make sure to zigzag the needle evenly so the two sides line up when you reach the top.

Shrinky Dink Jewellery

I used to make shrink art when I was a child – not that I ever actually made anything practical. Now, though, shrink plastic sheets come in lots of colours, and I have the knowhow to make all sorts of wonderful things. It's wondrous stuff: you can stamp on it, draw on it, punch holes in it and cut it into any shape you want. I like to gather trinkets from friends, flea markets and the back of the junk drawer to cluster with shrink shapes on a charm necklace.

TIME

THIS IS A QUICK PROJECT – I SPEND FAR LONGER PLANNING THE DESIGNS THAN ACTUALLY MAKING THE JEWELLERY. YOU COULD MAKE A FEW ITEMS IN ONE AFTERNOON.

MATERIALS

RUBBER STAMPS – REMEMBER THE PLASTIC SHRINKS TO SEVEN TIMES SMALLER THAN THE ORIGINAL, SO CHOOSE LARGE STAMPS

STAZON INK, OR OTHER INK PADS THAT YOU CAN USE ON PLASTIC

SHRINK PLASTIC (FOR STOCKISTS SEE PAGE 155)

FINE-POINT PERMANENT MARKER PENS

JEWELLERY FINDINGS: EARRING FIXINGS, NECKLACE CHAINS, CLASPS, JUMP RINGS, RING BASES

TOOLS

PENCIL

SCISSORS

HOLE PUNCH

TWO FLAT BAKING TRAYS

ALUMINIUM FOIL

JEWELLERY PLIERS

DESIGN THE NECKLACE OR EARRINGS

1. Choose the designs you would like to make. For the feather earrings I found real feathers and used these as inspiration for the shape. For the bracelet I printed a doily stamp design.

2. If you are using stamps, first print the shapes onto the shrink plastic. Dab your chosen stamp onto the inkpad firmly and evenly, but don't press too hard, as you want to get ink only on the raised sections.

3. Place the shrink plastic on a flat, hard surface. Then firmly press your inked stamp onto the plastic, making sure you apply even pressure across the whole stamp. (You'll see that the shrink plastic has a matt side and a shiny side. I think the effect is slightly nicer on the shiny side, but it's a matter of preference.)

4. Lift the stamp straight off, being careful not to smudge the inked design. Allow the ink to dry; 10 minutes should be enough. Repeat the above process for all the stamped designs you would like to make.

5. If you're simply outlining a shape, as with the feathers, then draw this with a pencil (see Figure 1). If you're drawing your own pattern to appear on the jewellery, use a fine-point permanent marker so that it won't rub off.

6. When all the designs are dry, use the scissors to carefully cut out your shapes. Use the hole punch to make a hole where you'd like to attach a chain for a necklace, or where you will attach the earring fixings.

SHRINK YOUR SHAPES

1. Preheat your oven to medium (160°C/320°F/gas mark 3). If you have a fan-assisted oven, use the setting without a fan, to ensure your shapes don't fly around.

2. Place the shapes on a piece of foil on a flat baking tray, and put them in the preheated oven until you see the plastic has shrunk and flattened. It will start to curl up first, but don't worry – it will flatten back down when it's ready. If you have different colours of shrink plastic, they may take different lengths of time (anything from 15 seconds to a minute) to shrink and flatten, in which case bake them in batches.

3. When you remove the shapes from the oven, press down on them with the other baking tray to make sure they are completely flat. Be careful, though, as the tray that has been in the oven will be hot!

4. Using your jewellery pliers, open a jump ring and thread it through the hole in the shrink shape, then through the necklace chain or earrings (see Figure 2). Close the jump ring using the pliers.

5. If you'd like to add more items to your jewellery – such as for a charm bracelet or necklace – you can attach them with more jump rings in the same way, or thread them straight on if they already have holes or loops.

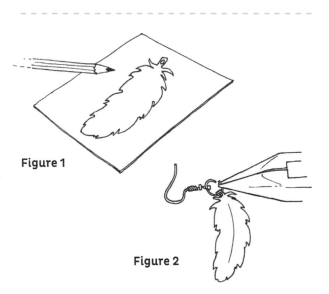

Figure 1

Figure 2

TIPS

It's a good idea to draw your designs on paper first, to minimise mistakes when you come to make the real thing.

You can trace designs straight onto the plastic if you choose the transparent variety. Be careful not to smudge your designs as you go.

summer camisole

TIME

THIS IS QUITE AN IN-DEPTH PROJECT. YOU'LL NFED TO SET ASIDE AT LEAST A WEEKEND.

It's so satisfying to wear something you've made yourself. Lovely Sarah, who teaches lots of our Makery workshops, studied lingerie design, so she created this pattern for us. I love the contrast of the neon ribbon against the delicate fabric. For tips on sewing with a pattern see the guide on page 150.

TOOLS

PATTERN PIECES PROVIDED AT THE BACK OF THE BOOK

PAPER SCISSORS

PINS

FABRIC SCISSORS

SEWING MACHINE

TAPE MEASURE

IRON

SAFETY PINS X 2

LIGHTER OR MATCHES

MATERIALS

CAMISOLE FABRIC: 100CM X 110CM (40IN X 44IN) LIGHTWEIGHT MATERIAL, SUCH AS A DELICATE PRINTED COTTON

RIBBON FOR THE STRAPS AND TIES: 250CM (99IN) X 0.5CM TO 1CM (⅛ TO ¼IN) WIDE

ELASTIC: UP TO 38CM (15IN) X 1CM (¼IN) WIDE – SEE INSTRUCTIONS ON PAGE 36 FOR DIFFERENT SIZINGS

CO-ORDINATING POLYESTER THREAD

PREPARE YOUR PATTERN

1. Decide which pattern to use – Small to Medium (UK 8-12/US 6-10, marked in a dotted line), or Medium to Large (UK 12-16/US 10-14, shown with a solid line). The elasticated back means that each pattern will fit a range of sizes. Cut out the pattern pieces provided.

2. Pin each pattern piece onto your fabric, making sure you align the arrow on the pattern with the grain of the fabric. (For details on aligning with the grain, see page 150.) Cut out. Use pins to transfer the markings for the centre front neck opening.

3. Set your machine to straight stitch, length 2.5.

MAKE THE FRONT SECTION

1. Cut 8cm (3in) down the centre front neck edge as shown on the pattern, also cutting 1cm (¼in) into the corners diagonally. With the right side of the fabric upwards, fold the three snipped edges backwards, towards the wrong side, along the dotted lines, to create an open rectangle. Pin and iron. Stitch around the rectangle with a 0.5cm (⅛in) seam allowance, to give a neat finish on the front (see Figure 1).

2. Fold the two top front edges of the camisole backwards, towards the wrong side, by 1cm (¼in), then by another 2cm (¾in). Pin and iron. Stitch in place with a 1.5cm (½in) seam allowance. This will give you two 'tubes' through which to thread your ribbon.

3. Cut the ribbon into four pieces, 2 x 75cm (30in) long (for the straps) and 2 x 44cm (17½in) long (for the front ties).

4. Attach a safety pin to each of the shorter pieces of ribbon and thread these through the two tubes. Pull the ribbon all the way through, so you have two long ends that poke out in the middle. The other ends of the ribbon should be flush with the fabric edges at the sides. Machine stitch these ends to the fabric to secure them in place and remove the safety pins. (See Figure 2, over the page.)

5. Singe the ends of the loose ribbon by wafting a lighter or match flame over them for a split second; this will help to stop them from fraying.

6. Now for the underarm edges. With the right side of the fabric upwards, fold a double 1cm (¼in) seam towards the wrong side on each underarm. Pin and iron flat, then stitch in place with a scant 1cm (¼in) seam allowance, just catching the fabric in place.

Figure 1

SEW THE BACK AND SIDES

1. With the right side of the fabric upwards, take the top edge of the camisole back piece, and fold over backwards, towards the wrong side, by 1cm (¼in), then by another 2cm (¾in). Pin and iron, then stitch in place with a 1.5cm (½in) seam allowance to create a tube as you did on the front.

2. Take your elastic – 32cm (12¾in) for UK 8-10 (US 6-8), 34cm (13½in) for UK 10-12 (US 8-10), 36cm (14½in) for UK 12-14 (US 10-12), 38cm (15in) – and attach a safety pin to each end. Anchor one end to the fabric at the end of the tube, and thread the other end through the tube using the safety pin to help you. The elastic is shorter than the fabric, so you'll find the fabric will gather slightly. Pull the elastic so that it pokes out from each side by 1cm (¼in) and use the safety pins to secure it. Machine stitch the elastic in place at each side and remove the safety pins.

3. With right sides facing, line up the front and back side seams – ensuring the front and top back edges match up perfectly (if the bottom edges are slightly mismatched, that's OK). Pin together and stitch with a 1cm (¼in) seam allowance.

4. Switch your machine to zigzag stitch, medium length and width. Sew down the side seams, in between the stitching and the raw edge, to help stop the edges fraying.

FINISH THE HEM

1. If there is any discrepancy in the lengths of the camisole front and back, trim the bottom edge so that the side seams line up.

2. Turn up the bottom edge towards the wrong side by 1cm (¼in), and then by another 2cm (¾in). Pin and iron in place. Switch your machine back to straight stitch (medium length), and sew in place with a 1cm (¼in) seam allowance.

ATTACH THE STRAPS

1. Pin one end of each long piece of ribbon to the inside of the camisole, aligning them with the front points shown on the pattern with an X. Stitch in place.

2. Then cross them over and pin the other end to the top back seam – positioning them 11cm (4¼in) from the side seams (gathered length). Slip the camisole on and check the shoulder straps are the correct length for you. Adjust accordingly if not, then stitch in place.

3. Tie the front loose ribbon ends in a bow to finish.

Figure 2

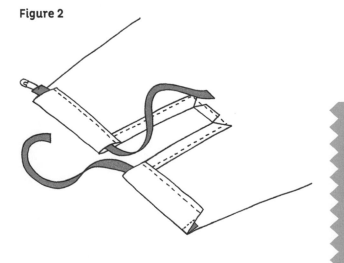

TIPS

If you'd like to make a feature of the stitching, try using a contrasting coloured thread.

You could add loops to the sides of the cami and thread ribbon through to turn it into a belted style top.

vintage tape measure brooch

When The Makery first opened, Zoë, one of our original staff members, made us each a brooch to wear on our aprons. Customers admire them so often, I thought I would include how to make one. I can't be certain I've got Zoë's technique exactly as she did it, but this is my way, and the easiest I've tried. If you're lucky enough to find a vintage tape measure lurking in an old sewing box, this is a perfect way to show it off. Otherwise try using ribbon or strips of thin leather.

TIME

ONCE YOU GET YOUR HEAD AROUND THE FOLDING PART, THIS IS A REASONABLY QUICK PROJECT. YOU COULD COMPLETE IT IN ONE EVENING.

TOOLS

NEEDLE

EMBROIDERY SCISSORS

MATERIALS

CO-ORDINATING POLYESTER THREAD

VINTAGE TAPE MEASURE: 100CM (40IN) – OR LENGTH OF RIBBON OR LEATHER

BROOCH BACK

GLUE

FOLD THE OUTER RING OF YOUR BROOCH

1. Thread your needle and tie a large knot at the end (see page 148).

2. Take the end of the tape measure and fold it as shown in Figure 1, in a clockwise direction, to create a point. The end of the point should be around 4cm (1¾in) from the centre point (where the tape crosses itself).

3. Grip the tape measure in the centre with one hand. Holding the long end of the tape in the other, repeat the fold (again clockwise) to create another point opposite the first. Again, the tape will cross over itself in the middle.

4. Grip that point, and then take your needle and thread, and make a stitch through the layers of tape to hold them in place. Continue the same process – folding the tape clockwise to create more points, and stitching them in place in the centre – until you have seven points, completing your outer ring. (See Figure 2.)

FOLD THE INNER POINTS AND FINISH

1. Once you have the outer ring, you can start making another round of points just inside the first set. For this, repeat the folding and stitching process, but the points will be roughly 2.5cm (1in) from the centre. Continue until you have four of the smaller points.

2. To finish, make a loop with the tape, folding it back on itself and tucking the end under. You will need to trim the end off, and finally stitch in place, securing the thread at the back of the finished rosette.

3. Glue the brooch clasp to the back of the rosette and leave to dry.

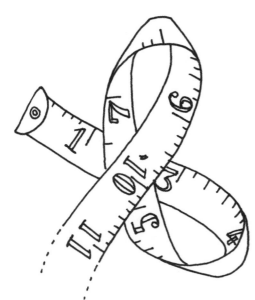

Figure 1

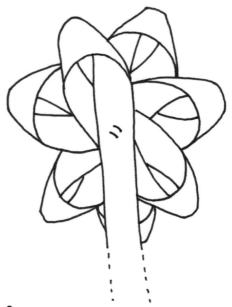

Figure 2

TIP

With practice these rosettes are fairly quick. You could make them larger or smaller, and use them for a variety of purposes, from hair accessories to wrist corsages, or as gift decorations for a crafty friend.

SUNGLASSES CASE

A little while ago I discovered these brilliant flex-frames and they are perfect for creating purses, clutch bags and, as here, cases for glasses or sunglasses. You push the sides of the frame, and it opens, giving a professional-looking case with no chunky fastenings.

TIME

ALLOW A COUPLE OF EVENINGS FOR THIS PROJECT.

MATERIALS

OUTER FABRIC: 2 X PIECES, EACH MEASURING 14CM X 25CM (5½IN X 10IN)

LINING FABRIC: 2 X PIECES, EACH MEASURING 14CM X 25CM (5½IN X 10IN)

WADDING: 2 X PIECES, EACH MEASURING 14CM X 21CM (5½IN X 8¼IN), OR USE COTTON BATTING (SEE PAGE 155 FOR STOCKISTS)

CO-ORDINATING POLYESTER THREAD

11.4CM (4½IN) FLEX-FRAME

TOOLS

PINS

SEWING MACHINE

IRON

FABRIC SCRAP OR TEA TOWEL

HAMMER

MAKE THE POUCH

1. Lay one of the pieces of outer fabric on top of a piece of lining fabric, right sides facing. Pin along the top, short edge and machine stitch to make one half of the case, leaving a 1cm (¼in) seam allowance. Repeat for the other pair of pieces, then turn both halves right side out, and iron flat.

2. Place the wadding under a piece of scrap fabric or a tea towel, and iron to bond the fibres.

3. Place a piece of wadding, or batting, on the wrong side of one of the outer fabric pieces, making sure the bottom edges line up. Pin in place. Repeat with the other half. (See Figure 1.)

4. Open out the two sides of the case, and lay one side on top of the other, so that the right sides of the outer fabric are facing, and the right sides of the lining are facing, and they all match up. Pin together.

5. Machine stitch down each side and across the bottom of the outer fabric, starting and finishing 2.5cm (1in) down from the seam joining it to the lining. (See Figure 2.)

6. Then machine stitch down each side (not across the bottom) of the lining fabric, beginning 2.5cm (1in) down from the top seam of stitching.

7. Turn the pouch right side out through the gap left at the bottom of the lining.

8. Turn the two bottom edges of the lining fabric into the inside, by 1cm (¼in). Pin and machine top-stitch in place, 0.2–0.3cm (⅛in) from the edge.

9. Push the lining into the outer pouch – the case should start to take shape at this point. Coax in the fabric around the gaps at the top side seams so that the folded edge lines up with the seam. Iron once you have created a neat rectangle.

10. Pin the outer to the lining on each side (see Figure 3). Then machine stitch a line across the width of one half, from one side edge to the other side edge, 2cm (¾in) down from the top. The stitching should be through one side of the pouch only. Repeat for the other half. This should give you a tube through which to feed the flex-frame.

FIX IN THE FLEX-FRAME

1. Open out the flex-frame and feed one end through the tube on one side, and the other end through the other tube. You'll find it easier if you do both at the same time. (See Figure 4.)

2. Once you've fully fed the frame through the tubes, line up the hinges, and force the pin or screw supplied with the frame through the holes. I find it easier to use a hammer for this!

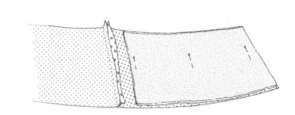

Figure 1

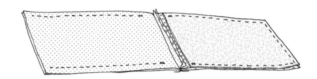

Figure 2

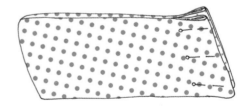

Figure 3

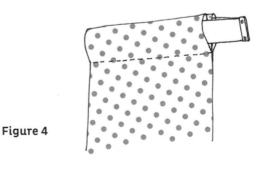

Figure 4

44

TIP

You may find the flex-frame a little
time-consuming to put together the first
time you try. It will get easier and quicker
each time you practise.

compact mirror & CASE

The perfect addition to any girl's handbag, this compact mirror and case makes a thoughtful gift. If you pick fabric that particularly suits the lucky recipient, you can make it especially personal.

TIME

THE MIRROR IS PRETTY QUICK TO MAKE, AND THE CASE TAKES A LITTLE LONGER, SO AIM TO HAVE THE PROJECT COMPLETED IN A COUPLE OF EVENINGS.

MATERIALS

CIRCULAR MIRROR: 7.5CM (3IN) DIAMETER (SEE PAGE 155 FOR STOCKISTS)

PIECE OF THICK FELT: 10CM X 10CM (4IN X 4IN) SQUARE

SCRAP OF MEDIUM OR LIGHTWEIGHT IRON-ON INTERFACING: UP TO 10CM X 10CM (4IN X 4IN) SQUARE. PLUS 10CM X 20CM (4IN X 8IN) IF YOU'RE USING FABRIC RATHER THAN OILCLOTH FOR THE CASE; SEE INSTRUCTIONS

SCRAP OF FABRIC FEATURING AN ATTRACTIVE MOTIF: UP TO 10CM X 10CM (4IN X 4IN) SQUARE

FABRIC OR OILCLOTH FOR THE CASE: 10CM X 20CM (4IN X 8IN)

CONTRASTING POLYESTER THREAD

TOOLS

ERASABLE FABRIC PEN OR TAILOR'S CHALK

FABRIC SCISSORS

IRON

PINS

SEWING MACHINE

FABRIC GLUE

SMALL FISHING WEIGHT OR SIMILAR

MASKING TAPE (IF YOU'RE USING OILCLOTH)

TAPE MEASURE

BACK THE MIRROR

1. Lay the mirror on the felt, and draw around it. Carefully cut out around your line.

2. Iron the interfacing onto the back of your motif fabric scrap, following the instructions on the pack. Neatly cut out the fabric motif and pin it to the felt circle in your desired position. Machine stitch in place with a scant 0.5cm (⅛in) seam allowance (see Figure 1). The interfacing will mean the fabric shouldn't fray.

3. Lay the mirror reflective side down on your work surface and apply glue to the back. Stick the felt in place on it, wrong side down. I like to put a weight on the felt while it's drying, to be sure of a secure stick.

MAKE THE CASE

1. If you're using fabric for the case, iron the interfacing onto the back. If you're using oilcloth, you can skip this stage.

2. Cut a small crescent shape from the middle of one of the short ends of fabric or oilcloth, about 2cm (¾cm) long and 0.5cm (⅛in) deep, so you can pull the mirror out of the case more easily. Machine stitch across both short ends of the fabric, going around the crescent, with a 0.5cm (⅛in) seam allowance. This is not only for decorative purposes – it will strengthen the fabric and reduce the risk of stretching. (See Figure 2.)

3. Fold the fabric or oilcloth in half, wrong sides together. Pin in place if you're using fabric, or tape it with masking tape if you're using oilcloth. Machine stitch down the two side seams to hold the case together. Ensure you reverse at the start and end of each line of stitching to hold it securely.

4. Once the glue on the mirror is dry, slip it into the case.

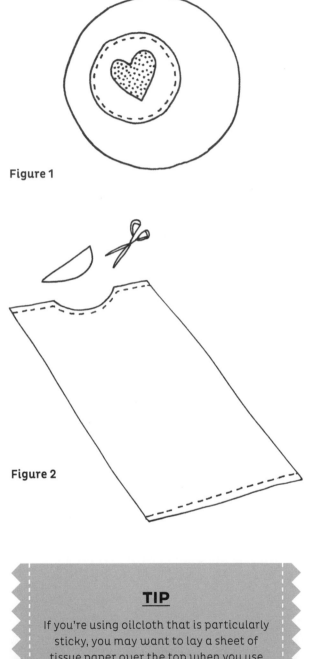

Figure 1

Figure 2

TIP

If you're using oilcloth that is particularly sticky, you may want to lay a sheet of tissue paper over the top when you use your sewing machine to stitch. This will ensure the oilcloth flows freely through it. Simply tear the tissue paper off when you've finished.

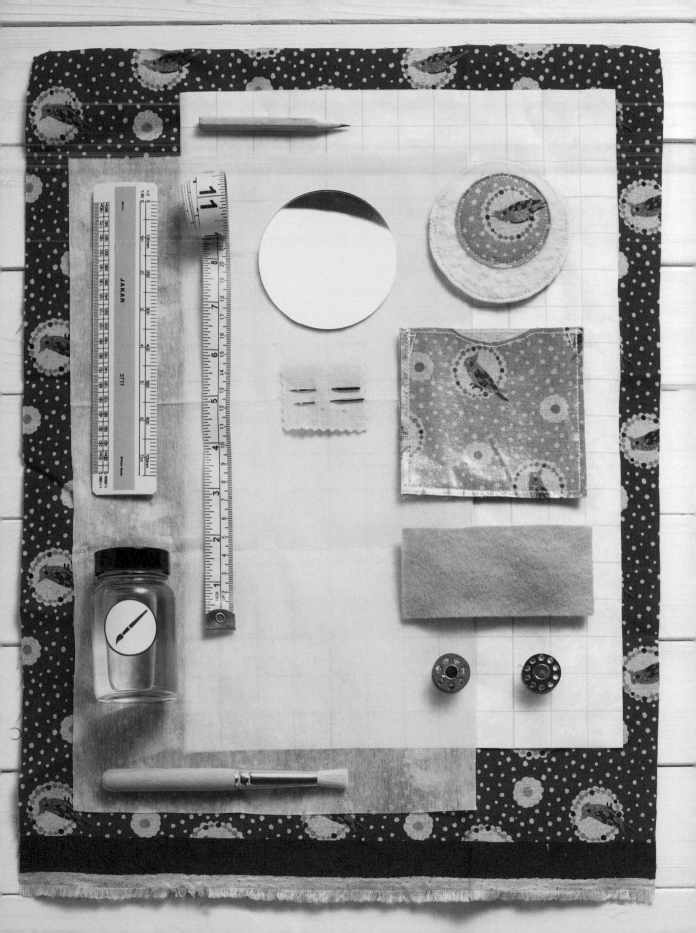

ShOuLdeR BaG

A girl can never have too many bags! Plus, I think they're a brilliant way to show off your favourite fabrics. This design is a different take on the tote bag – the shape is 'puffy' so you can fit lots in it. Think about how you position the pattern piece on the fabric, to get the best effect – here, I've taken advantage of the broad contrasting stripe.

TIME

YOU COULD PROBABLY FINISH THIS IN A COUPLE OF AFTERNOONS OR EVENINGS, PROVIDED YOU'RE NOT INTERRUPTED.

MATERIALS

OUTER FABRIC FOR BAG AND HANDLES: 65CM X 110CM (26IN X 44IN)

LINING FABRIC: 50CM X 110CM (20IN X 44IN)

MEDIUM-WEIGHT IRON-ON INTERFACING

CO-ORDINATING POLYESTER THREAD

TOOLS

PATTERN PIECE PROVIDED AT THE BACK OF THE BOOK

TAPE MEASURE

FABRIC SCISSORS

SEWING MACHINE

PINS

IRON

LARGE SAFETY PIN

SEW THE OUTER AND LINING

1. Cut two pattern pieces from the outer fabric, and two from the lining fabric. Cut two handle pieces of 11cm x 110cm (4 ½in x 44in) each from the outer fabric. On each bag piece, mark the two dots on the bottom edge, and points A, B, C and D, with pins.

2. Set your machine to the longest straight stitch, and machine a line between the two dots along the bottom edge of each piece of fabric (outer and lining), ensuring you leave long tails of thread at each end.

3. Take one piece of fabric and hold the ends of thread. Pull on the ends gently to gather the fabric so that the gathered section measures 12cm (4¾in) from dot to dot (see Figure 1). Repeat with the other three pieces of fabric.

4. Pin the two outer pieces of fabric together, right sides facing. Set your machine to a medium-length straight stitch and sew from point A to point B around the long curved base of the bag, leaving a 1.5cm (½in) seam allowance. Repeat for the lining pieces. Clip the curves and turn the outer bag pouch right side out.

PUT THE BAG TOGETHER

1. With the lining wrong side out, sit the outer bag pouch inside the lining pouch, so that the right sides of the two pouches are facing. Pin together at the curved side seams. Machine stitch from C to D at each side with a 1.5cm (½in) seam allowance (see Figure 2). Clip the curves.

2. Turn the bag right side out, so that the lining sits inside the outer fabric. Iron flat the side seams you've just sewn and trim the top edges if necessary: the outer and lining should match up on each side of the bag, and should be in a straight line.

3. Take one side of the bag, and fold the top (straight) edge towards the inside by 1cm (¼in) –use a tape measure if you need to. Iron flat. Fold again, in the same direction, by another 5cm (2in). Iron and pin in place. Machine stitch with a 4.5cm (1¾in) seam allowance 0.5cm (⅛in) from the bottom of the fold (see Figure 3) to create a tube, securing the ends by reversing. Repeat for the other side.

MAKE THE HANDLES

1. Iron interfacing to the back of each handle piece. Fold a 1cm (¼in) hem down both long edges of each handle, towards the wrong side. Iron flat.

2. Fold each handle in half lengthways, wrong sides facing. Iron flat. Machine stitch, with a 0.5cm (⅛in) seam allowance.

3. Attach a safety pin to the end of one handle and use this to thread it through one of the tubes. Match the two ends of the handle together, overlapping them by about 5cm (2in). Secure by making three lines of machine stitching to hold them together securely. Repeat for the other handle in the other tube.

4. Gather the bag on the handles to make that fantastic puffy effect.

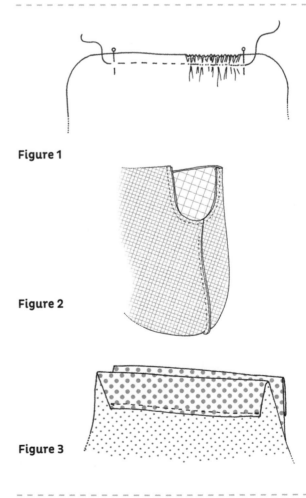

Figure 1

Figure 2

Figure 3

TIP

If you think you're going to carry heavy loads in your bag, I would do two lines of stitching for the outer pouch so that the bag is as strong as it can be.

CARD WALLET & PASSPORT CASE

These two projects are great for anyone on the move. By choosing appropriate fabrics you can make them as a gift for a male or a female (or a co-ordinating set for both!). The card wallet is slim and handy to carry tickets and bank cards, while the passport case on page 59 gives your documents a home and some personality.

TIME

BOTH PROJECTS ARE SIMILAR IN LENGTH; I'D SAY AN AFTERNOON OR TWO EACH.

TOOLS

TAPE MEASURE

RULER

ERASABLE FABRIC MARKER OR TAILOR'S CHALK

FABRIC SCISSORS

IRON

PINS

SEWING MACHINE

KNITTING NEEDLE

CARD WALLET
MATERIALS

OUTER FABRIC: 2 PIECES, MEASURING 24CM X 11CM (9½IN X 4½in) AND 10CM X 11CM (4IN X 4½IN)

MEDIUM-WEIGHT IRON-ON INTERFACING: 2 PIECES, MEASURING 24CM X 11CM (9½IN X 4½in) AND 10CM X 11CM (4IN X 4½IN)

POCKET FABRIC: 2 PIECES, EACH MEASURING 23CM X 12CM (9IN X 4¼IN)

CORD ELASTIC: 26CM (10¼IN)

CO-ORDINATING POLYESTER THREAD

MAKE THE CARD WALLET

1. Iron the larger piece of interfacing to the back of your large piece of outer fabric. Then iron the smaller piece of interfacing to the back of your small piece of outer fabric.

2. Take one of the pocket pieces and fold over 0.5cm (⅛in) along one of the long (23cm/9in) edges, to the wrong side. Pin and iron in place. Repeat for the other pocket piece. Note that if your fabric has a top and a bottom to the pattern, make sure one hem is along the left-hand side and the other hem is along the right-hand side.

3. Now take one of the pocket pieces and fold it into a concertina as shown in Figure 1. Pin and iron the folds, and then machine stitch them in place down each side with a 0.25cm (⅛in) seam allowance. You'll be stitching through three layers of fabric in places, so take your time. Repeat for the other pocket piece.

4. Fold the elastic in half and knot the cut ends together. Pin the knotted end in the centre of the large outer fabric (on the right side), along one of the short edges (see Figure 2). Stitch in place with a 0.25cm (⅛in) seam allowance.

5. Now lay the large outer fabric piece in front of you, right side facing up. Take one of the pocket pieces and lay it on top, right sides facing, with the short (11cm/4½in) raw edges lined up and the neat (folded) pocket edge facing the centre. You should have one pocket piece at either end of the outer fabric piece. Finally, place the lining fabric piece on top (with the right side facing down) in the centre. Pin in place, and curve the four outer corners. (See Figure 3.)

6. All the other edges should pretty much line up. If they don't, trim them. Machine stitch all the way around the four outer edges with a 0.5cm (⅛in) seam allowance.

7. Clip the corners (see page 150) and turn the wallet right side out through one of the gaps in between the pockets and lining fabric. Use a knitting needle if required to push out the corners.

8. Once the wallet is neatly turned out, iron it all flat.

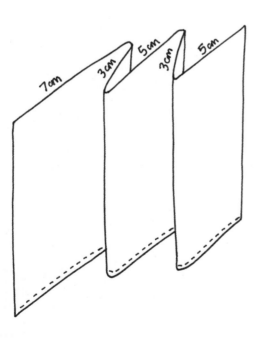

Figure 1

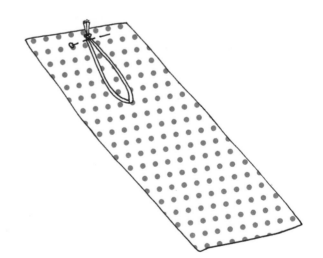

Figure 2

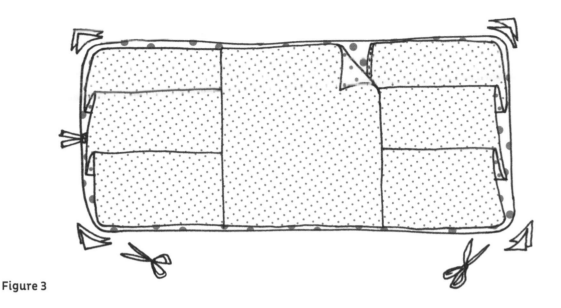

Figure 3

PASSPORT CASE MATERIALS

FOR A 12.5CM X 9CM (5IN X 3¾IN) PASSPORT:
OUTER FABRIC: 16.5CM X 22CM (6½IN X 8¾IN)

MEDIUM-WEIGHT IRON-ON INTERFACING:
16.5CM X 22CM (6½IN X 8¾IN)

LINING FABRIC: 16.5CM X 10CM (6½IN X 4IN)

POCKET FABRIC:
PIECE 1: 16.5CM X 9CM (6½IN X 3¾IN)
PIECE 2: 32.5CM X 9CM (12¾IN X 3¾IN)

CORD ELASTIC: 23.5CM (9¼IN)

CO-ORDINATING
POLYESTER THREAD

FOR OTHER PASSPORT SIZES

OUTER FABRIC: HEIGHT OF PASSPORT +
4CM (1¾IN) X DOUBLE THE WIDTH OF YOUR
PASSPORT + 4CM (1¾IN)

MEDIUM-WEIGHT IRON-ON INTERFACING:
SAME AS FOR OUTER FABRIC

LINING FABRIC: HEIGHT OF PASSPORT + 4CM
(1¾IN) X 10CM (4IN)

POCKET FABRIC:
PIECE 1: SAME HEIGHT AS OUTER FABRIC X
ACTUAL WIDTH OF PASSPORT
PIECE 2: SAME HEIGHT AS OUTER FABRIC + 16CM
X ACTUAL WIDTH OF PASSPORT

CORD ELASTIC:
DOUBLE WIDTH OF PASSPORT + 2CM (¾IN)

CO-ORDINATING
POLYESTER THREAD

MAKE THE PASSPORT CASE

1. First you need to measure your passport, as they come in a variety of sizes. Measure from top to bottom (height) and from one side to the other (width). If your passport has a height of 12.5cm (5in) and width of 9cm (3½in) you can simply use the measurements that are given. Otherwise, remember to adjust to the fabric sizes as described on page 59.

2. Iron interfacing to the back of your outer fabric. With your scissors, curve the corners very slightly – just to take the points off.

3. To make the pockets, sit them vertically, trim the points off the two left-hand corners of the smaller piece, and the two right-hand corners of the larger piece.

4. Now for the lining. Switch your sewing machine to zigzag and stitch down the two long sides of fabric, along the edges – this is to ensure they don't fray.

5. Now you have all your fabric pieces measured and prepared, it's time to start constructing. Take the the large pocket piece and fold the left-hand long edge over by 1cm (¼in) towards the wrong side. (This is the edge you have not trimmed the corners on.) Pin and iron in place. Set your sewing machine back to sew straight and stitch with a 0.5cm (⅛in) seam allowance.

6. Fold the large pocket piece into a concertina, as shown in Figure 1 for the card wallet on page 58, but with the following dimensions (from the top): Xcm, 3cm (1in), 7cm (2¾in), 3cm (1in), Xcm. Here, Xcm is the leftover fabric length divided by 2; so for a 12.5cm (5in) high passport, the extra would be 4.75cm (1¾in) top and 4.75cm (1¾in) bottom. These folds will form the pockets. Pin and iron the folds in place.

7. Machine straight stitch down each long edge with a 0.5cm (⅛in) seam allowance, to hold the pockets in place. At times you'll be sewing through three layers of fabric, so take your time.

8. Now take the small pocket piece and fold the right-hand long edge over by 1cm (¼in) towards the wrong side (the edge you have not trimmed the corners on). Pin, iron and machine stitch in place with a 0.5cm (⅛in) seam allowance.

9. Fold the elastic in half and knot the two cut ends together nice and tightly. Place the outer fabric piece in front of you, right side facing up, and position the elastic on top, with the knotted end halfway down the left-hand edge (as in Figure 2 for the card wallet on page 58). Machine stitch in place.

10. With the outer fabric still in front of you, right side facing up and the elastic on the left-hand side, start positioning the other pieces. Take the small (unfolded) pocket piece and place on top of the outer fabric with the right sides facing, so that the right-hand curved corners line up with each other. Pin in place.

11. Now take the pleated pocket piece and place on top of the outer fabric with the right sides facing, so that the left-hand curved corners line up. Pin in place.

12. Finally, take the lining piece and place it on top of the outer fabric, right side facing down (it will cover part of the front and back lining). The top and bottom edges should line up, and the central lining should sit centrally on the whole thing (similarly to Figure 3 for the card wallet). Pin in place.

13. Machine stitch all the way around all four edges with a 1cm (¼in) seam allowance. If you need to trim some of the edges slightly to ensure they are aligned, that's fine. Clip the curved corners (see page 150). Turn the whole thing right side out through one of the gaps between the lining. Use a knitting needle if required to push out the corners.

14. Once the wallet is neatly turned out, iron flat.

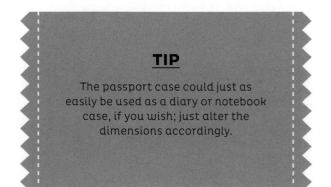

TIP

The passport case could just as easily be used as a diary or notebook case, if you wish; just alter the dimensions accordingly.

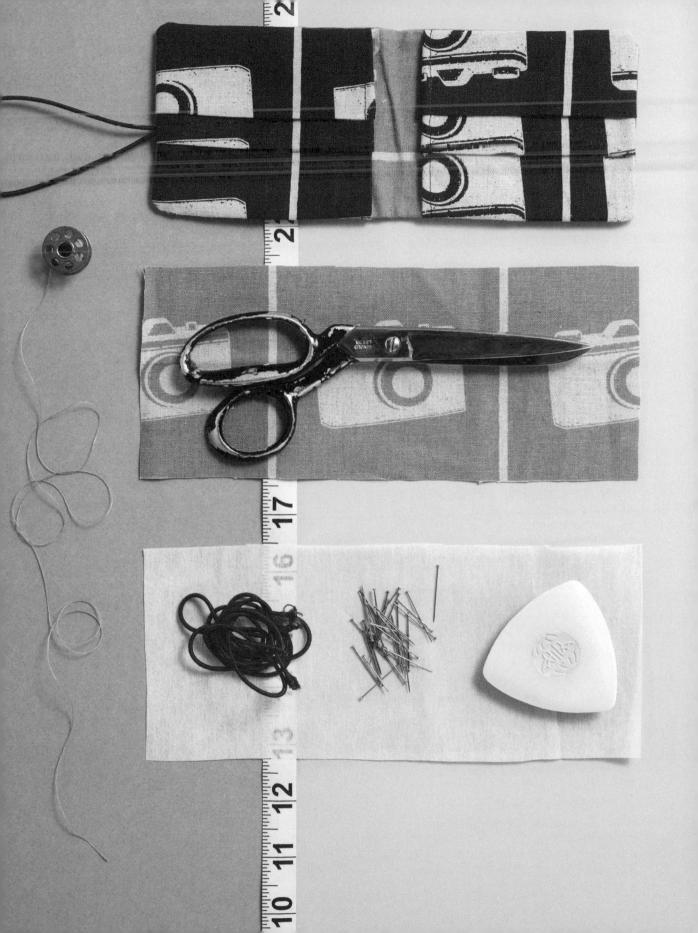

MAKE-UP ROLL

I'm not the sort of girl who always carries a make-up bag. I do, however, like to have things readily accessible when I want them and I hate having to root around in my handbag. This make-up roll is a great solution. It could equally serve as a pouch to store paintbrushes or pens and pencils. Try using oilcloth for the main fabric lining to help keep the make-up roll clean. You can even make your own – see page 93.

TIME

ALLOW AT LEAST TWO EVENINGS TO COMPLETE THIS PROJECT.

MATERIALS

WADDING: 21CM X 25CM (8¼IN X 10IN), OR USE COTTON BATTING (SEE PAGE 155 FOR STOCKISTS)

LINING AND BINDING FABRIC: 50CM X 110CM (20IN X 44IN)

OUTER FABRIC: 21CM X 25CM (8¼IN X 10IN)

CO-ORDINATING POLYESTER THREAD

TOOLS

IRONING BOARD

FABRIC SCRAP OR TEA TOWEL

IRON

FABRIC SCISSORS

PINS

TAPE MEASURE

RULER

ERASABLE FABRIC PEN OR TAILOR'S CHALK

FABRIC SCISSORS

SEWING MACHINE

NEEDLE

MAKE THE BRUSH POCKET

1. Place the fabric scrap or tea towel over the wadding and iron on a medium setting to bond the wadding fibres.

2. Cut the following pieces from the lining fabric: 21cm x 25cm (8¼in x 10in; main lining), 14cm x 25cm (5½in x 10in; pocket lining), 100cm x 6cm (40in x 2¼in; binding) and 4cm x 30cm (1¾in x 12in; fastening tie).

3. Fold over the top (long) edge of the pocket lining by 1cm (¼in), towards the wrong side, then fold again by another 1cm (¼in). Pin, iron and machine stitch in place 0.75cm (¼in) from the folded edge.

4. Place the wadding, or batting, in front of you horizontally. Lay the main lining fabric on top, with the right side facing up. Now lay the pocket lining fabric on top, right side facing up, aligning the bottom and side (raw) edges. Pin through all three layers to hold them in place.

5. Machine stitch in vertical lines 2-3cm (1in) apart, from the top to the bottom of the pocket lining fabric, securing the ends by reversing. These lines of stitching create the tubes for your make-up brushes. You could mark the places where you want to sew with a ruler and erasable fabric pen or tailor's chalk.

ADD THE OUTER FABRIC AND TIE

1. Take your fastening tie fabric, fold one of the short ends in towards the wrong side by 1cm (¼in) and iron in place. Now fold the fabric in half lengthways, wrong sides facing. Iron. Open out and fold each long edge towards the middle, lengthways, before re-closing the ironed fold. Again, iron in place. Now machine stitch down the full length of the fabric, with a 0.25cm (⅛in) seam allowance.

2. Take the lining and pocket and lay so that the wadding is uppermost. Place the outer fabric on top with its right side up. Pin in place.

3. Position the tie fastening onto the outer fabric, halfway up the right-hand side edge. Line up the short, unfolded edge with the raw edge of the outer fabric. Pin in place.

4. Set your machine to the longest stitch setting and machine stitch all the way around each edge with a 0.5cm (⅛in) seam allowance. (See Figure 1.)

BINDING AND FINISHING

1. Fold the binding in half lengthways, wrong sides facing. Lay the make-up roll flat in front of you with the outer fabric upwards. Starting in the middle of the bottom edge, lay the binding on top (still folded in half), lining up the raw edges. Pin along to the first corner. Machine stitch with a 1cm (¼in) seam allowance, making sure you stop stitching 1cm (¼in) before reaching the corner. Secure your stitching and remove the fabric from the machine. (See Figure 2.)

2. Fold the binding at the corner, and pin down the length of the second side in exactly the same way. Machine stitch from the folded edge down the side, again stopping 1cm (¼in) before the end. Repeat until you're back where you started. Trim the binding end so there's a 1cm (¼in) overlap. (See Figure 3.)

3. Fold the binding over the raw edges of the roll. Turn under the raw edge of the binding so that it just covers all the stitching (about 1cm/¼in). Pin in place all the way around the four sides of the roll, then slip-stitch in place by hand.

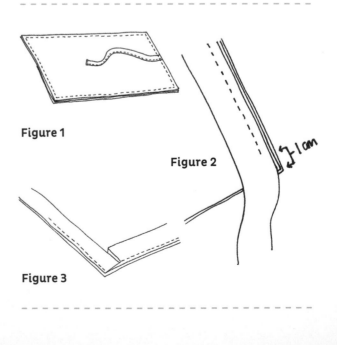

Figure 1

Figure 2

1cm

Figure 3

TIP

If your make-up brushes are different thicknesses you can vary the distance between your vertical lines. You don't have to keep them evenly spaced as long as they are between 2cm and 3cm (around 1in) apart.

Knitted Cup Cuff

TIME

THIS IS A SIMPLE, QUICK PROJECT THAT SHOULDN'T TAKE MORE THAN ONE EVENING.

This makes a super gift for someone who regularly orders 'coffee to go'. Gone is the need for a cardboard cuff – this cup cuff is not only a stylish accessory, but better for the environment, too. The button is a real feature, so choose something to appeal to the person you're giving it to. If you're a knitting beginner, see the guide to getting started and understanding knitting instructions on page 152.

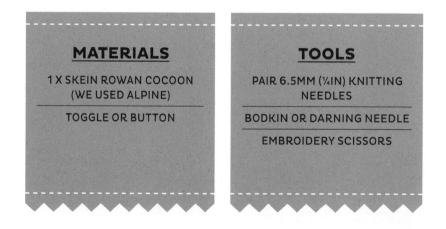

MATERIALS

1 X SKEIN ROWAN COCOON (WE USED ALPINE)

TOGGLE OR BUTTON

TOOLS

PAIR 6.5MM (¼IN) KNITTING NEEDLES

BODKIN OR DARNING NEEDLE

EMBROIDERY SCISSORS

KNIT THE CUFF

1. Cast on 38 stitches. Depending on the tension of your stitches, this should give a cuff that fits around a standard paper coffee cup, so check after a few rows that it is the right size. You don't want to pull the yarn too tight, or make the cuff too big, either, as it needs to be a little elastic to fit on the cup and then grip it snugly.

2. You will need to increase (written as inc) the number of stitches in some rows. To do this, at the beginning or end of the row, work into the front of the stitch first, and then into the back of the same stitch – so making two stitches out of one. On a row that starts with a knit stitch, knit into the front of the stitch as normal, then before slipping if off the needle, knit again into the back of the stitch (see Figure 1). Then slip the stitch off. For a row that begins with a purl stitch, use the same method, but in this case purl into the front then the back of the stitch.

3. Then knit the cuff as follows:
   *K1, P1; repeat from * to end of row.
   Repeat this row for 3 more rows.
   Inc 1, *P1, K1; repeat from * to last stitch. Inc 1.

   *K1, P1; repeat from * to end of row.
   Repeat this row for 2 more rows.
   Inc 1, *P1, K1; repeat from * to last stitch. Inc 1.

   *K1, P1; repeat from * to end of row.
   Repeat this row for 3 more rows.
   Cast off leaving a long tail of yarn.

4. Bring the two short ends together and sew up the seam. To do this, thread the tail of yarn into your bodkin or darning needle and pass the needle through the opposite bottom corner to your finishing point, to anchor the sides together.

5. Find the first vertical column of V-shaped stitches on each side. Pull the Vs apart gently so that you can see a series of bars between the stitches, like a ladder.

6. Thread your needle under the first bar on the left-hand side, and then across and under the first bar on the right. Continue up the rest of the seam in this way, in a zigzag pattern. About halfway up, and then again at the top, pull the yarn tight to close the seam. (See Figure 2.)

7. At the top, secure the yarn and weave in the end. Then turn the cuff right side out and sew the toggle or button in place.

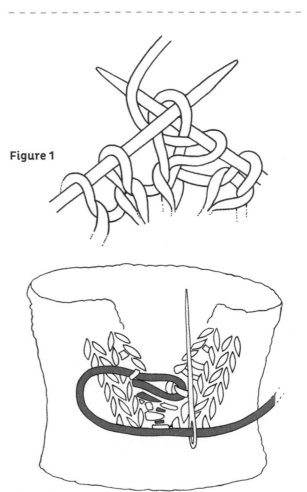

Figure 1

Figure 2

TIP

You can really change the look of this cute cuff by altering the embellishment. I've gone for a classic look with a toggle, but you could use a polka-dot button or a mother-of-pearl heart, or even embroider an initial or a message if you have the time!

TOY TRUCK PINCUSHION

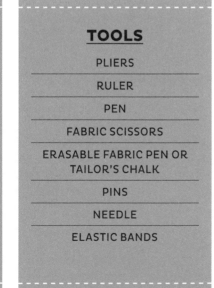

TIME

YOU WON'T NEED ANY MORE THAN AN AFTERNOON TO MAKE THIS QUICK PROJECT.

I have made lots of pincushions in teacups and eggcups – and it has made me think about what other receptacles I could use to create this crafter's essential. A trip to a flea market gave me the idea of using vintage toy trucks. Not only are they interesting and unique to look at, they also inject an element of fun into a crafting session – just whiz the little truck across the table to your friend!

MATERIALS

A VINTAGE TOY TRUCK – THE SORT WITH A PLASTIC TRAILER OR ROOF

BLOCK OF FOAM – NO MORE THAN 3CM (1IN) DEEP

FABRIC: 20CM X 20CM (8IN X 8IN)

CO-ORDINATING POLYESTER THREAD

SUPER GLUE

TOOLS

PLIERS

RULER

PEN

FABRIC SCISSORS

ERASABLE FABRIC PEN OR TAILOR'S CHALK

PINS

NEEDLE

ELASTIC BANDS

PREPARE THE TRUCK

1. Pull the trailer or roof off the truck. If it won't come with a good tug, use a pair of pliers. It doesn't matter if the odd small piece of plastic remains on the base – it will be covered up when you attach your fabric-covered block of foam.

2. Precisely measure the rectangular cargo-carrying area of the truck, then use the pen to mark the dimensions on the foam, and use the scissors to cut out this shape carefully.

CONSTRUCT THE PINCUSHION

1. Now for a little maths to calculate the fabric size. Add 10cm (4in) to your rectangle measurements – both to the width and to the length. For example, if your rectangle is 5cm x 3cm (2in x 1in), your fabric needs to be 15cm x 13cm (6in x 5in). Mark these dimensions on your fabric with tailor's chalk (or draw a paper template and pin this on), then cut the fabric to the appropriate size.

2. Lay the fabric in front of you lengthways, wrong side up. Place the foam in the middle of the fabric, also lengthways. Fold up one long side of fabric and wrap it around the foam block, then fold up the other (opposite) side of fabric and wrap it around so that the two sides of fabric meet, or at least almost meet. Stretch the fabric around the foam reasonably tightly and pin it in place (see Figure 1). Secure the two edges together with ladder stitch (see page 149).

3. Repeat the process with the short ends of fabric, ensuring you fold the corners neatly as you go, rather as you would make a bed. (See Figure 2.) Again, pin and then stitch securely to hold in place. You should now have a fabric-covered block of foam. It will be quite untidy underneath if it's anything like mine, but should be relatively neat on top.

4. Spread a thin layer of glue onto the bottom of the truck's trailer or cargo area, paying particular attention to the edges. Lay the fabric-covered foam on top, or push it in, and hold in place with the elastic bands while the glue dries.

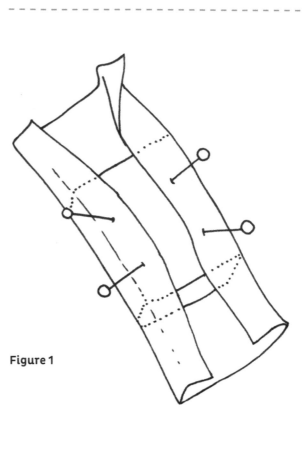

Figure 1

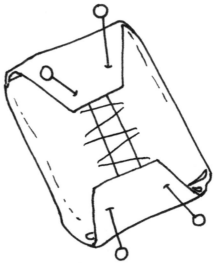

Figure 2

TIP

If you can't get hold of
a foam block, a new
dish-washing sponge
would work just as well.

100 m

Great
**Yarmouth
Mercury**

Tablet case

Those favourite geek gadgets deserve a stylish cover to keep them safe when travelling. This case is padded to make it nice and squidgy for extra protection. It's a great technique that can be adapted to any size – make it larger for laptops or smaller for e-readers and phones. I've included size alteration instructions, along with actual dimensions for an iPad. I use the one photographed all the time, and I love it.

TIME

THIS IS A FAIRLY STRAIGHTFORWARD PROJECT. IT SHOULD TAKE THREE TO FOUR HOURS IF YOU'RE FREE FROM DISTRACTIONS.

MATERIALS

OUTER FABRIC FOR IPAD: PIECE 1 = 59CM X 23CM (23¼IN X 9IN); PIECE 2 = 20CM X 23CM (8IN X 9IN) – OR SEE MEASUREMENTS OVER THE PAGE FOR OTHER DEVICES)

LINING FABRIC FOR IPAD: 59CM X 23CM (23¼IN X 9IN)

WADDING FOR IPAD: 52CM X 23CM (20½IN X 9IN), OR USE COTTON BATTING (SEE PAGE 155 FOR STOCKISTS)

CO-ORDINATING POLYESTER THREAD

2 X VELCRO PIECES, EACH ROUGHLY 1CM X 1CM (½IN x ½IN)

TOOLS

FABRIC SCISSORS

IRON

PINS

SEWING MACHINE

EMBROIDERY SCISSORS

NEEDLE

MAKE THE TABLET CASE

1. If you're making a cover for a device other than an iPad, follow the alteration guide below.

2. Once you have cut out the fabric you need, iron all the pieces.

3. Next take your wadding, if using, and lay a piece of fabric over it and iron that too, using a medium heat setting, to bond the wadding fibres and make it easier to work with. Make sure the iron doesn't touch the wadding itself.

4. Take your large outer fabric piece and match the top short end with the top short end of the lining fabric, right sides facing. Pin the two pieces together and sew along this short end with a 1cm (¼in) seam allowance.

5. Open the pieces out, and place the wadding, or batting, on the wrong side of the lining, matching a short end to the seam you have just sewn. Pin in place. Sew a straight line 1cm (¼in) into the wadding, parallel to your previous seam, to hold the wadding in place.

6. Now take your smaller piece of outer fabric, and iron under a 1.5cm (½in) hem along the bottom short end, then turn over another 1.5cm (½in) and iron again. Stitch the hem in place with a 1cm (¼in) seam allowance.

7. Next open out the large piece of fabric with lining and wadding attached and fold the outer fabric right over so that it sandwiches the wadding and you have all the right sides of fabric facing out. Iron it flat.

8. Lay this piece in front of you with the outer fabric facing up and the neat hem closest to you. Fold up the neatly finished bottom edge away from you by the full length of the tablet plus 1cm (¼in) and pin in place.

9. Lay your smaller piece of outer fabric on top, right side down, matching the top raw edges, and pin in place (see Figure 1). Stitch around the three unfinished sides (the two sides and top), making sure you catch all the layers and leaving a 1cm (¼in) seam allowance. Trim all four corners at 45°, and trim the wadding down the two side edges if it has become bulky.

10. Now for the magic! Turn the case right side out, and press it one last time – doesn't it look lovely! Finally, fold the top flap over and hand stitch the velcro to the two corners of the flap and the corresponding points on the case. Try to make sure you sew through only one layer on the flap, so the stitching isn't visible from the right side.

MEASUREMENTS FOR OTHER DEVICES

FOR DEVICES OTHER THAN THE IPAD, PLEASE FOLLOW THESE INSTRUCTIONS:

FIRST TAKE THE FOLLOWING DIMENSIONS): WIDTH / LENGTH / DEPTH

THEN MEASURE OUT YOUR FABRIC PIECES AS FOLLOWS:

OUTER FABRIC: PIECE 1 = (WIDTH + TWICE THE DEPTH + 3CM/1IN) X (LENGTH X 2.5)

OUTER FABRIC: PIECE 2 = (WIDTH + TWICE THE DEPTH + 3CM/1IN) X (LENGTH X 85%)

LINING FABRIC: (WIDTH + TWICE THE DEPTH + 3CM/1IN) X (LENGTH X 2.5)

WADDING OR BATTING: (WIDTH + TWICE THE DEPTH + 3CM/1IN) X (LENGTH X 2 + 4CM/1¼IN)

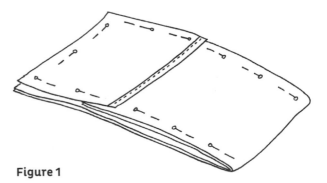

Figure 1

TIP

If, when you stitch the velcro to the flap, you do go through all the layers of fabric so that the stitching is visible from the right side, you could use decorative buttons to hide the stitching.

MONOGRAM KEYRING

A keyring is such a useful gift to receive, and I wanted to include something that you could personalise for the person you're giving it to. Then it struck me: I have a really old monogram keyring that I love, so why not produce a tactile, contemporary version using some gorgeous fabric?

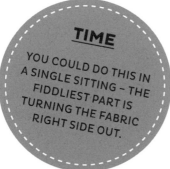

TIME

YOU COULD DO THIS IN A SINGLE SITTING – THE FIDDLIEST PART IS TURNING THE FABRIC RIGHT SIDE OUT.

MATERIALS

SMALL PIECE LIGHTWEIGHT FABRIC (SUCH AS 100% COTTON): 10CM X 20CM (4IN X 8IN)

NARROW RIBBON FOR LOOP (NO MORE THAN 0.5CM/ ⅛IN WIDE): 6CM (2¼IN)

CO-ORDINATING POLYESTER THREAD

POLYESTER TOY STUFFING

KEYRING (THE SPLIT RING TYPE)

CONTRASTING POLYESTER THREAD

TOOLS

LETTER TEMPLATE PROVIDED AT THE BACK OF THE BOOK

PENCIL (OPTIONAL)

TRACING PAPER (OPTIONAL)

FABRIC SCISSORS

PINS

SEWING MACHINE

KNITTING NEEDLE (OR SOMETHING SIMILARLY LONG AND POINTED)

NEEDLE

SEW YOUR KEYRING

1. If you think you might want to reuse the alphabet letter templates, trace the letter you need onto a piece of tracing paper and cut out your copy. If, on the other hand, you intend to use the letter just this once, you can cut directly from the templates.

2. Fold your piece of fabric in half with right sides facing, and pin your letter template to it. Cut around the template. If your chosen letter has a hole in it (eg. a, b, d, etc), trace the shape of hole onto the fabric and stitch the line using small running stitch with contrasting thread (see page 148). Repeat for the back piece of fabric. Now replace the fabric pieces together, right sides facing. Pin, then stitch in place.

3. Fold the ribbon in half and position it between the two layers of fabric at the point shown on the template, with the loop on the inside and the raw edges of the ribbon lined up with the raw edges of your fabric. Pin in place (see Figure 1).

4. Machine stitch around the outside edge of your letter with a 0.5cm (⅛in) seam allowance, leaving a gap between the notches as shown on the template. If you have created your own template, leave a gap 2cm (¾in) wide in a suitable position.

5. Clip the curves and trim the corners, being careful not to touch your stitching line (see Figure 2). Then turn the letter the right way out – you may need to use the knitting needle for this step, as some letters can prove quite fiddly. Pack your letter with toy stuffing so that it's tight and the letter holds its shape firmly. Use ladder stitch (see page 149) to hand stitch the gap closed.

6. Attach the split ring keyring to the ribbon loop.

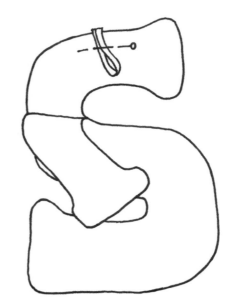

Figure 1

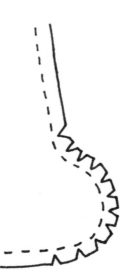

Figure 2

TIP

The internet is a wonderful source of alternative letter styles to create your own templates. Or you could find a letter you like in a pattern book, or draw one freehand.

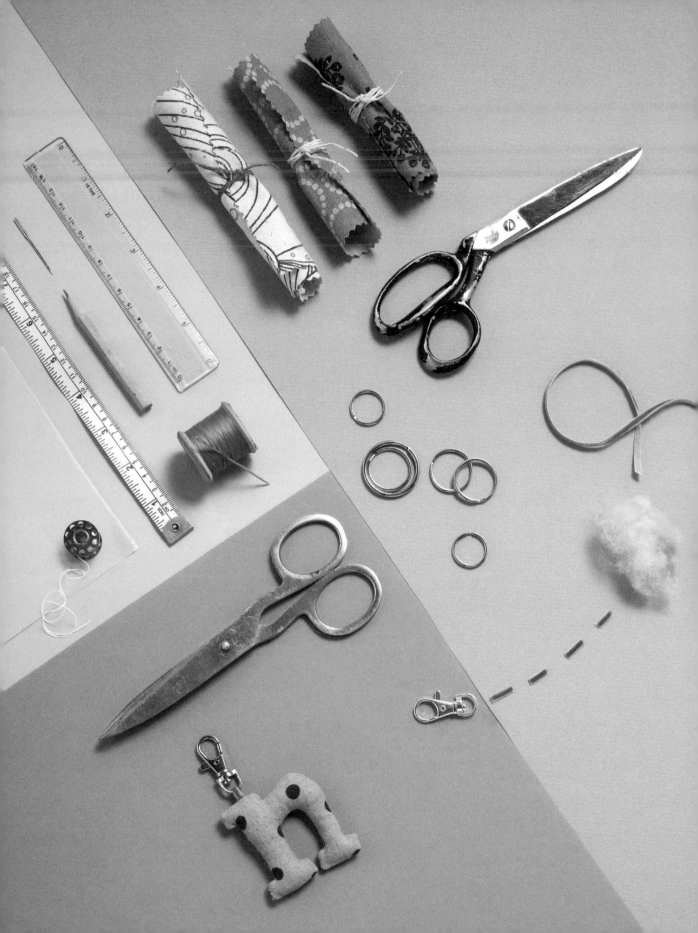

DECORATED TAGS

TIME

IF YOU HAVE ALL THE BITS AND BOBS TO HAND, THIS IS A SUPER-QUICK PROJECT.

I've been making tags for many years. I use them on gifts, for labelling jars and as decorations. There are myriad ways to embellish the basic design – here, I've given you just a few ideas to pick and choose from. I like to think it's these sorts of simple touches that people really notice.

TOOLS

PAPER SCISSORS

IRON

HOLE PUNCH

PENCIL

DOUBLE-SIDED TAPE

SUPER GLUE

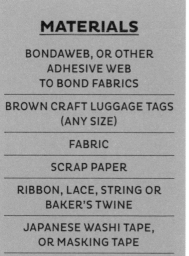

MATERIALS

BONDAWEB, OR OTHER ADHESIVE WEB TO BOND FABRICS

BROWN CRAFT LUGGAGE TAGS (ANY SIZE)

FABRIC

SCRAP PAPER

RIBBON, LACE, STRING OR BAKER'S TWINE

JAPANESE WASHI TAPE, OR MASKING TAPE

BUTTONS

FABRIC-BACKED TAGS

1. Cut a piece of Bondaweb just larger than the size of the tag and choose a piece of fabric that is also just larger than the tag. Lay the Bondaweb glue side down onto the back of your fabric. Iron in place using a medium iron.

2. Place a scrap of paper onto your ironing board (this will prevent you ruining your ironing-board cover). Lay the tag on the paper. Peel the paper layer off the Bondaweb-backed fabric, and lay this glue side down onto the tag, so that the glue completely covers the tag. You should have the patterned side of the fabric facing up at this point. Iron over the fabric to ensure it's firmly stuck to the tag.

3. Peel the fabric-backed tag off the scrap paper, and carefully trim the fabric so that it neatly matches the size and shape of the tag. Use your hole punch to make a hole at the pointed end of the tag, and thread through your chosen ribbon, or piece of lace or string.

FABRIC MONOGRAM TAGS

1. Cut a piece of Bondaweb to roughly the same size as the tag and choose a piece of fabric that is the same size. Lay the Bondaweb glue side down onto the back of your fabric. Iron in place with a medium iron.

2. Now draw the mirror image of the letter you want to appear on the finished tag onto the paper side of the Bondaweb. Practise drawing the letter backwards on a scrap of paper beforehand if you like, or cut out the letter the right way round from a scrap of paper, then flip it, and use this as a template.

3. Cut out the letter shape from your fabric, then peel off the paper layer. Lay the letter onto your tag and gently iron it in place.

WASHI TAPE OR MASKING TAPE TAGS

1. Lay strips of decorative masking tape haphazardly across your tag in all directions. Where pieces end halfway across I like to tear rather than cut the tape, for a less uniform style. (See Figure 1.)

2. Neatly cut the ends of the masking tape around the edges of your tag.

RIBBON AND BUTTON TAGS

1. Cut several strips of ribbon and back them with double-sided tape. Apply the ribbon to your tags, trimming the ends so that the ribbon is flush with the edges of your tag.

2. Choose some co-ordinating buttons and put a dab of glue on the back of each. Stick them in place on the tags.

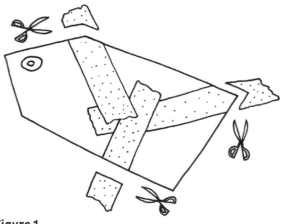

Figure 1

TIP

Washi tape is a decorative masking tape from Japan. It comes in all kinds of colours and patterns, from geometric designs to florals and birds. You can find this and other decorative masking tapes easily online. See page 155 for stockists.

Hand-Carved Rubber Stamps

Stamping is a brilliant way to decorate cards, fabric, tags and so on. I'd toyed with the idea of making my own stamps for a while, and now that I have I'm hooked! Begin with the simplest designs. Keep practising, working up to more difficult designs as you hone your carving skills – you will be amazed at the results. I am planning on printing a large piece of fabric and making a skirt . . . one of these days.

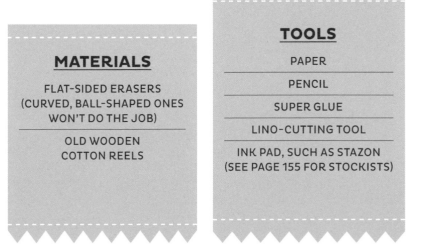

TIME

EACH STAMP WILL TAKE ANYTHING FROM HALF AN HOUR TO A COUPLE OF HOURS, DEPENDING ON HOW AMBITIOUS YOU ARE.

MATERIALS

FLAT-SIDED ERASERS (CURVED, BALL-SHAPED ONES WON'T DO THE JOB)

OLD WOODEN COTTON REELS

TOOLS

PAPER

PENCIL

SUPER GLUE

LINO-CUTTING TOOL

INK PAD, SUCH AS STAZON (SEE PAGE 155 FOR STOCKISTS)

MAKE YOUR STAMPS

1. Choose your design – make your first attempt something simple, such as a heart shape – and sketch it onto paper.

2. Copy the design onto the eraser and then carefully carve away the areas that you want to remove. I begin at the sides and work my way in, then concentrate on the detail afterwards. Use a wider blade for removing the larger areas, and a fine blade for the detail. (See Figure 1.)

3. When you've finished, gently brush or blow away the excess pieces of rubber.

4. To make the stamp easier to hold, glue the eraser onto an old wooden cotton reel (see Figure 2).

5. Test out your stamp on some rough paper or a fabric offcut, depending on what you want to print onto (see Figure 3).

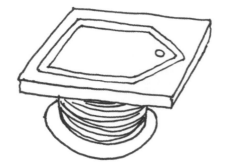

Figure 2

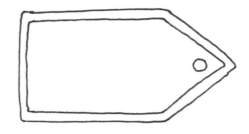

Figure 3

Figure 1

TIPS

The more intricate your design, the trickier it will be to carve. One of the easiest designs for me was the hot-air balloon – it doesn't have too many sharp curves, which are tricky.

A clean cut is essential, so make sure the blades for your carving tool are perfectly sharp.

LUNCH BAG

Packing up a lunch for yourself or someone else can be quite comforting and nostalgic. How cared for would you feel if it came in a specially handmade bag? I've tried to mimic the shape and style of a classic brown paper bag by making a flat-based shape with a pinking-sheared edge. Oilcloth is great to work with – no fraying – and it's wipe-clean. The inner bag is easy to remove, and I've included a tag to add a name label, or maybe brighten someone's day with a handwritten message. The bulldog clip fastening was a clear winner – I love its utilitarian chic.

MATERIALS

OILCLOTH LINING FABRIC:
56CM X 34CM (22IN X 13½IN)

OILCLOTH OUTER FABRIC:
56CM X 36CM (22IN X 14½IN)

OILCLOTH TAG FABRIC:
16CM X 7CM (6½IN X 2¾IN)

CO-ORDINATING AND CONTRASTING POLYESTER THREAD

BULLDOG CLIP

OPTIONAL EXTRAS

STAZON INKPAD

LETTER STAMPS

DRY-WIPE PEN

BAKER'S TWINE OR RIBBON:
35CM (13¾IN)

TOOLS

PINKING SHEARS

MASKING TAPE

SEWING MACHINE

PINS

FABRIC SCISSORS

TAPE MEASURE

ERASABLE FABRIC PEN OR TAILOR'S CHALK

MAKE THE LINING BAG

1. Trim the top 56cm (22in) edge of the lining oilcloth fabric with pinking shears.

2. Fold your oilcloth in half widthways, matching up the two short edges, with right sides facing. Don't pin the oilcloth before sewing as it will leave holes in the fabric. Instead I use masking tape to hold edges together.

3. Thread up your machine with matching thread and set to straight stitch, stitch length 2.5–3. Stitch down the side and along the bottom with a 1cm seam allowance to create a pocket.

4. Now create the flat base of the bag. Put your hand inside the (inside-out) bag and flatten out one of the corners to make a triangle, with the side seam that you have just sewn running down the middle of the triangle (see Figure 1). Secure with a pin (this time it won't matter if your pin marks the oilcloth as the point will be discarded).

5. With your pen or tailor's chalk, mark a line horizontally across the triangle, measuring 8cm (3¼in) from edge to edge (see Figure 1). This line really does need to be horizontal, or your lunchbag will be a bit wonky. Machine stitch along the line, securing by reversing (see page 151). Cut off the triangle point, leaving a 1cm (¼in) seam allowance. Repeat on the other corner.

MAKE THE OUTER BAG

1. Repeat steps 1–5 above, but with your outer oilcloth fabric. The only difference will be that your folded fabric in step 2 will be slightly larger.

2. To create the defined edges on the side-seams, take your outer bag and turn it right side out. Carefully crease the tall straight edges from the base to the top on all four corners of the bag. Finger-press the creases in place (see Figure 2).

3. Change to contrasting thread on your machine and carefully sew the length of these folds close to the edge – with a 0.2cm (¹⁄₁₆in) seam allowance – from the base to the top. Have a practice on a scrap first. To get a nice even line of stitching, line up the folded edge with a line on the plate

below the presser foot. Reverse stitch at the start and end of each line to secure your sewing (see page 151).

4. Sit the lining bag inside your outer bag, making sure the two bags fit together comfortably. To finish, fold over the top of your bag and secure the fold with the bulldog clip!

MAKE A TAG FOR YOUR BAG

1. Fold the fabric in half widthways, with wrong sides together, so you have a rectangle 8cm x 7cm (3¼in x 2¾in). Take your baker's twine, fold it in half and place the folded end between the layers of your tag at the top. Then stitch around the outside, all four edges, leaving a 0.3cm (¹⁄₁₆in) seam allowance.

2. Using your letter stamps and Stazon ink, stamp a name or message on to the back of the tag. (Alternatively you could leave it blank for a message written in a dry-wipe pen.) When the ink is dry, tie the loose ends of baker's twine to the bulldog clip.

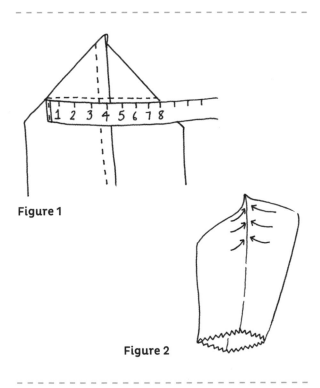

Figure 1

Figure 2

TIP

You can make your own oilcloth using 'Iron-on vinyl'. Simply iron the vinyl onto the fabric of your choice; cottons and linens work best. You can use it on both sides of the fabric, and it's washable. You can even experiment with catching lace underneath the vinyl – endless fun! See page 155 for stockists.

CUCKOO CLOCK

TIME

THIS IS QUITE A LENGTHY PROJECT, AS THERE ARE A FEW DIFFERENT TECHNIQUES INVOLVED. YOU SHOULD BE ABLE TO COMPLETE IT IN TWO OR THREE EVENINGS, BUT YOU COULD SPEND LONGER ON THE EMBROIDERY IF THE MOOD TAKES YOU!

When I was little, I was fascinated by the cuckoo clock in my playroom. I'd almost forgotten how much I loved that clock until I saw one recently at a flea market. This version doesn't have a working cuckoo, but it does tell the time and it's just enough to give a little sense of nostalgia.

TOOLS

PATTERN PIECES PROVIDED AT THE BACK OF THE BOOK

PENCIL

PAPER SCISSORS

BRADAWL OR PIN

DRILL (OPTIONAL)

FABRIC SCISSORS

PINS

DOUBLE-SIDED TAPE

ERASABLE FABRIC PEN OR TAILOR'S CHALK

EMBROIDERY NEEDLE

RULER

MATERIALS

MOUNT BOARD (THE TYPE USED FOR PICTURE FRAMING): 25CM X 25CM (10IN X 10IN)

PIECE OF BACKING FABRIC: 25CM X 25CM (10IN X 10IN)

FELT SQUARE: 25CM X 25CM (10IN X 10IN) – WE USED GREY 4MM (⅛IN) THICK 100% WOOL HANDMADE FELT

CONTRASTING EMBROIDERY THREAD (FOR CLOCK DETAIL)

3MM-WIDE VELVET OR OTHER RIBBON: 45CM (18IN)

2 X FELT BALLS AND 2 X FELT HEARTS, OR BEADS

SCRAP OF CONTRASTING FELT: 5CM X 5CM (2IN X 2IN)

CONTRASTING EMBROIDERY THREAD (FOR FELT SCRAP)

CLOCK MECHANISM (SEE PAGE 155 FOR STOCKISTS)

BATTERY FOR CLOCK

MAKE THE CLOCK

1. Cut out the smaller cuckoo-clock pattern and trace around it onto the mount board. Mark the centre of the clock face – where you will attach the clock mechanism – using a bradawl or pin. Cut out the cuckoo-clock shape from the mount board carefully. Keep the template, as you will use it again later.

2. Using the bradawl or a drill, make a 0.6cm (⅛in) wide hole in the marked spot on the mount board. Note that you need to be precise with this step to ensure that the clock hands align perfectly.

3. Pin the larger cuckoo-clock pattern from the template onto your piece of fabric, and cut it out.

4. Stick double-sided tape around the edges of the back of the mount board. Peel off the top layer of the tape and lay the fabric on top, right side facing up. Stick it in place. The fabric should be 1cm (¼in) larger than the mount board all the way round.

5. Clip the fabric at all corners (see Figure 1). Turn over the mount board, and again stick double-sided tape around the edges. Peel away the top layer from the tape, fold the edges of the fabric over and stick in place. Take care at the corners to keep them neat.

6. Take the smaller cuckoo-clock pattern again and pin it onto the felt square, positioning it so you will have enough leftover felt for the leaves. Cut out.

FINISH THE DETAILS

1. Transfer the cuckoo door outline and clock-face markings (including the centre marking where the mechanism will fit through) onto the felt with pins or tailor's chalk. With your contrasting embroidery thread, stitch the door and clock face (but not the centre marking) using backstitch and French knots (see page 106). Make a hole at the centre marking on your felt with the bradawl.

2. Trace the cuckoo-clock leaves onto your leftover pieces of felt. Embroider the leaf markings on to each leaf using backstitch. Stitch the leaves to the clock, ensuring these stitches aren't noticeable from the front.

3. Cut the ribbon into two pieces, one 15cm (6in) long and one 30cm (12in) long. Stitch the felt hearts, balls or beads onto the end of each length of ribbon and secure them in place. Stitch the ribbon to the back of the clock at the bottom, so that they hang down. Make sure they are evenly spaced, so your clock isn't lopsided.

4. Trace the cuckoo shape onto the contrasting felt, and cut it out. Stitch the features using your second colour of embroidery thread, and stitch the cuckoo onto the clock face.

5. Stick double-sided tape around the edges of the messy side of the fabric-covered mount board (the side with the fabric folded over the edges). Peel off the top layer of the tape and position the felt cuckoo-clock face, being careful to align the centre hole of the clock face with the hole in the mount board. Stick down.

6. Assemble the clock mechanism according to the instructions that came with it and attach it through your clock face. Put in a battery (rechargeable if possible) and there's your hand-crafted cuckoo clock!

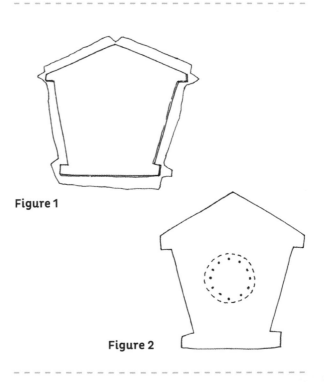

Figure 1

Figure 2

TIP

If you prefer you could use fabric instead of felt. You'll need to interface it though, to ensure it doesn't fray.

Decoupage Tins and Pots

I love arranging things! And what better receptacles than these tins. You can make a set for your crafty bits, another for your kitchen, and one for your stationery. Choose a selection of tins and pots – the sort that you don't need to open with a can-opener so there are no sharp edges.

TIME

ONE OF THE FASTER PROJECTS, THIS SHOULD BE DO-ABLE IN AN AFTERNOON.

MATERIALS

TINS AND POTS, CLEANED THOROUGHLY

PAPER (WE'VE USED VINTAGE MAPS AND MUSIC MANUSCRIPT)

DECOUPAGE ALL-IN-ONE GLUE AND SEALER, SUCH AS MOD PODGE MATT (SEE PAGE 155 FOR STOCKISTS)

SPRAY FIXATIVE (OPTIONAL, SEE PAGE 155 FOR STOCKISTS)

TOOLS

RULER

PENCIL

TAPE MEASURE

PAPER SCISSORS

PAINTBRUSH: 1CM (¼IN) DIAMETER OR SMALLER

MEASURE UP YOUR COVERING PAPERS

1. Take a pot and, using the ruler, measure the precise height of the side. If there is a slight lip at the top and bottom, ensure your measurements start and finish within the lip. Note down the measurement – this becomes your template height. (See Figure 1.)

2. Wrap the tape measure around the circumference of the tin. Add 1cm (¼in) to this measurement and note it down – this becomes your template width.

3. Take your chosen paper. Using the pencil and ruler, carefully draw a rectangle according to your height and width. Cut out the rectangle. The more accurate you are, the neater the finish will be. If you need to cut multiple pieces of paper to make up the size, that's fine – you can layer the paper.

GLUE AND SEAL YOUR TINS

1. Paint the surface of the tin with glue/sealer, ensuring a thin, even coat.

2. Carefully place the paper on top and smooth it out using your fingers. Apply more glue/sealer to the overlap, to glue it down. Leave the glued paper to dry for around 20 minutes. (Put the brush in water immediately after use, so that it doesn't dry and harden.)

3. You can leave your tins at that if you would prefer a rustic look. For a more hard-wearing finish, apply more coats of glue/sealer on top of the paper. You need to keep the coats thin and even and allow each one to dry before applying the next.

4. If you find the paper starts to wrinkle when you apply the top coats, which can happen with poor-quality paper, start again and spray the paper with fixative before you stick it. Or simply leave your decoupage tin without a top coat.

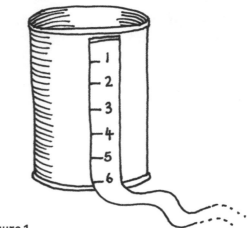

Figure 1

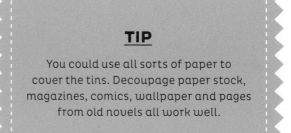

TIP

You could use all sorts of paper to cover the tins. Decoupage paper stock, magazines, comics, wallpaper and pages from old novels all work well.

EmbROidEREd bed linen

TIME

YOU'LL PROBABLY BE ABLE TO COMPLETE A PILLOWCASE IN AN AFTERNOON.

I've always liked really pretty bed linen, but it can be terribly expensive. With this project, you can make your own – and in a reasonably short space of time if you don't want to get too complicated with your design. Pillowcases are quick, but if you like you can embroider onto a duvet cover, too. For a stylish effect keep the design nice and simple, but use a well-chosen colour palette.

MATERIALS

BED LINEN – PILLOWCASES OR DUVET COVER

EMBROIDERY SILKS

TOOLS

ERASABLE FABRIC PEN

EMBROIDERY HOOP

EMBROIDERY NEEDLE

EMBROIDERY SCISSORS

IRON

DESIGN AND PREPARE TO SEW

1. Copy, draw or trace your design onto freshly ironed linen. If you like, you can use the template at the back of the book.

2. Select your colour scheme and stitches. I used French knots, detached chain stitch hearts and running stitch (see page 148) for this design.

3. Fix the part of the fabric you want to work on into an embroidery hoop. Make sure that the fabric is drum-taut when it is secured in the hoop.

FRENCH KNOTS

1. Make a knot in your embroidery thread to prevent it pulling through (see page 148), then push the needle through from the underside to the top of the fabric.

2. Wind the looped embroidery silk around the end of your needle three times, quite tightly (see Figure 1). Hold your thumb on your non-stitching hand over these loops, then push your needle back into the fabric right next to where it emerged – making sure the threads under your thumb stay put – to create a knot on the thread (see Figure 2).

DETACHED CHAIN STITCH HEARTS

1. Knot the thread (see page 148) and bring the needle up through the fabric at the bottom point of your heart shape.

2. Make a loop with the thread and push the needle back down through the fabric next to the point it came up from. Then bring it back up around 0.5cm (⅛in) from the original point, at the top of your heart. Make sure the needle re-emerges in the middle of the large loop of thread (see Figure 3).

3. Pull the needle through the loop, making sure you don't pull the thread too tight. Then make a small tying stitch at the top of the heart by pushing the needle back down through the fabric right next to where it last came up, just to the other side of the loop (see Figure 4).

4. Repeat to form the other side of the heart.

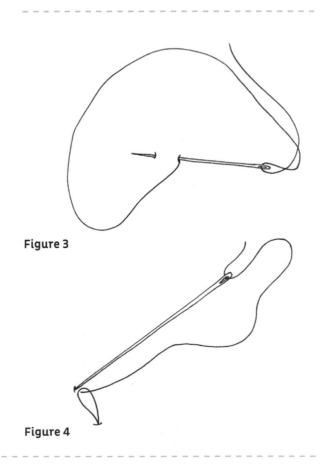

Figure 1

Figure 2

Figure 3

Figure 4

TIP

You could embroider
monogram letters to
personalise linen. Print
out your chosen font in
the required size and
trace onto the fabric.

Tile COASTERS

TIME

THIS IS A REASONABLY FAST PROJECT – YOU SHOULD BE ABLE TO GET IT ALMOST FINISHED IN ONE SITTING. IF, LIKE ME, YOU WANT TO ADD SEVERAL LAYERS OF VARNISH, YOU'LL NEED TO RE-VISIT IT EVERY FEW HOURS OR DAYS TO FINISH IT COMPLETELY.

I reckon you can never have too many coasters and these are a novel way to use up old paper scraps. I've chosen vintage comics to decorate my tiles, but you could use pages from magazines or old books, old photos, wrapping paper, or old record sleeves – or just about anything that's made from paper.

MATERIALS

SMALL CERAMIC TILES: 10CM X 10CM (4IN X 4IN)

COMICS, MAGAZINES, OLD BOOKS OR PHOTOS TO DECORATE THE TILES

FELT

TOOLS

RULER

PENCIL

PAPER SCISSORS

ALL-IN-ONE GLUE, SEALER AND VARNISH, SUCH AS MOD PODGE MATT FINISH (SEE PAGE 155 FOR STOCKISTS)

PAINTBRUSH

FABRIC SCISSORS

FABRIC GLUE

CREATE YOUR COASTER

1. Measure your tiles to calculate what size you need to cut the paper. My tiles were 10cm x 10cm (4in x 4in), so I cut my paper 9cm x 9cm (3½in x 3½in) to allow for a border.

2. Cut the paper to the appropriate size, rounding the corners.

3. Use the paintbrush to apply a thin layer of all-in-one glue to the top of the tile, and fix on the paper (see Figure 1). Leave the glue to dry according to the instructions.

4. When the glue is dry, apply a layer of the all-in-one glue on the top of the paper, brushing it right to the edges of the tile to seal it completely (see Figure 2). Leave that layer to dry, and if you want an even stronger surface, repeat this step to apply a second sealing layer.

5. Cut a piece of felt to the same size as the paper and use the glue to stick it to the bottom of the coaster. Leave the glue to dry according to the instructions.

TIP

When choosing comic or magazine pages to use for your coasters, select pages that don't have a lot of text on the other side, as this can show through when you apply the all-in-one glue.

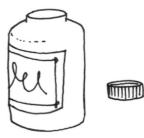

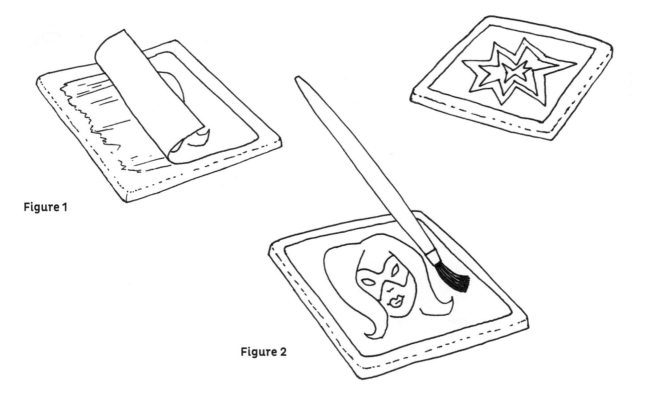

Figure 1

Figure 2

TIME

THIS PROJECT USES CHUNKY NEEDLES AND DOUBLE YARN, WHICH MAKES IT SPEEDIER THAN MOST KNITTING PROJECTS. IT TOOK ME A WEEK'S WORTH OF EVENINGS – BUT IF YOU'RE GOOD AT KNITTING, YOU'LL BE ABLE TO DO IT QUICKER.

CHUNKY RUG

When I dreamed this up, I imagined something irresistibly comfortable underfoot – and that's exactly what it is. Just take off your socks and let your feet snuggle in. I hadn't knitted for ages, but then an amazing knitting shop (woolbath.co.uk) opened nearby. Now knitting provides therapeutic activity as I unwind in front of the TV. If you're a beginner, see the guide to getting started and understanding knitting instructions on page 152.

MATERIALS

4 X SKEINS ERIKA KNIGHT MAXI WOOL (WE USED FLAX)

TOOLS

PAIR 20MM (¾IN) KNITTING NEEDLES

SCISSORS

DARNING NEEDLE

KNIT THE RUG

1. Find the ends of two of your balls of knitting yarn, knot them together and work with them as if they were one strand – using two balls at once will give you a chunkier finish.

2. Cast on 45 stitches. Depending on the tension of your stitches, this will give you a rug measuring approximately 75cm by 75cm (30in by 30in).

3. Knit the rug using moss stitch, as follows:
   Rows 1 and 4: K1, then bring yarn forwards and P1; then carry on repeating this along the row, and end with K1.
   Rows 2 and 3: P1, K1; then carry on repeating this along the row, and end with P1.
   For knitting methods, please refer to page 152.

4. Repeat rows 1 to 4 to repeat the pattern, until your rug measures 75cm (30in) long, knitting in the second pair of yarn balls when you need them.

5. Then cast off. Thread the ends of yarn into your work to conceal them.

TIP

There's a danger that the two balls of yarn will get tangled as you knit. To stop this happening, put each ball in a separate bowl on the floor.

Stag head

TIME

THIS IS QUITE A MEATY PROJECT – THINK OF HIM AS AN ONGOING TASK. (ALTHOUGH IF YOU'RE ANYTHING LIKE ME, YOU'LL TRY YOUR BEST TO COMPLETE HIM IN ONE SITTING RATHER THAN CONCENTRATE ON ANYTHING ELSE!)

I made a huge one of these for our Christmas window display one year at The Makery, and months later he was still up there! We have so many comments and requests for the pattern, I thought it was high time I shared him with you all. This stag is somewhat smaller than my original, but equally charming, I think.

MATERIALS

LIGHT TO MEDIUM-WEIGHT COTTON FABRIC: 50CM X 100CM (20IN X 40IN)

THIN FELT: 25CM X 50CM (10IN X 20IN)

COORDINATING POLYESTER THREAD

POLYESTER TOY STUFFING

10CM (4IN) EMBROIDERY THREAD

TOOLS

PINS

FABRIC SCISSORS

PATTERN PIECES PROVIDED AT THE BACK OF THE BOOK

SEWING MACHINE

KNITTING NEEDLE

ERASABLE FABRIC PEN OR TAILOR'S CHALK

LONG NEEDLE

MAKE THE ANTLERS AND EARS

1. Begin by cutting out all your felt and fabric pieces: 4 x antlers from the felt; 4 x ears, 2 x side heads, 1 x top head and 1 x back head from the fabric. Use pins to mark the ear positions and also points A and B on the side head pieces. Snip the notches on the side head and top head pieces. Use pins to mark the dots and the loop hanging position on the back head piece.

2. To make the antlers, first place one of the felt antler pieces on top of another and pin them together. Machine top-stitch all the way around the antler, leaving the bottom (straight) edge open – you need a very small seam allowance here, no more than 0.5cm (⅛in). Repeat with the other two felt antler pieces.

3. Now stuff the antlers. Gently push the stuffing in, a little at a time. You'll find it very hard to poke the stuffing all the way into the ends with your fingers, so use a knitting needle. The antlers need to be rigid enough to stand up. No one likes a floppy antler.

4. For the ears, place one pair of fabric ear pieces right sides together and machine stitch round the curved sides with a 1cm (¼in) seam allowance, leaving the straight edge open. Clip the corners to reduce some bulk, then turn ear the right way out. Again, you might need your knitting needle to help you. Pinch the ear in half at the open seam and tack together at the bottom with a couple of hand stitches. (See Figure 1.) Repeat for the other ear.

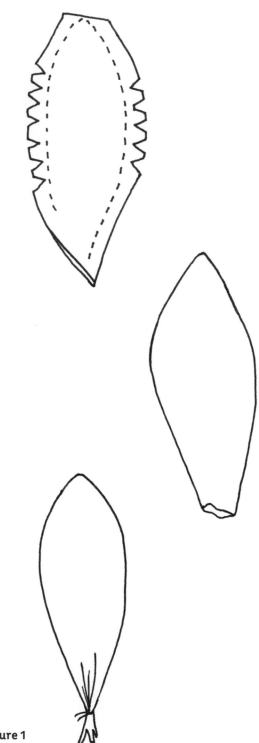

Figure 1

SEW AND STUFF THE HEAD

1. Take one finished ear and tack it to one of the side head pieces, as noted on the pattern, on the right side of the fabric with raw edges aligned. You need to ensure that the open side of the ear is facing towards the nose of the head piece. Repeat with the other ear and second side head piece.

2. Take the top head piece and pin it to one side head piece, right sides together, matching the notches and point A. Machine stitch in place with a 1cm (¼in) seam allowance. (See Figure 2.) Match the top head piece to the other side head piece, and again machine stitch in place, matching the notches.

3. Now machine stitch the two side head pieces together from the nose point around to the bottom of the neck, between the pins (points A to B on your pattern), leaving a 1cm (¼in) seam allowance.

4. Then machine stitch the two side head pieces together at the top, between points C and D. Pin and machine stitch in place with a 1cm (¼in) seam allowance.

5. Take the back head piece and pin it to the rest of the head, right sides together, all the way around the opening you've left at the back of the neck. Machine stitch in place with a 1cm (¼in) seam allowance, leaving a 10cm (4in) opening at the bottom. Clip all curves.

6. Turn the head right-side out and stuff it with polyester stuffing so that it's rigid enough to stay upright.

7. Hand stitch the opening in the bottom of the head with ladder stitch (see page 149). Position the antlers on the top of the stag's head, as noted on the pattern. Hand stitch in place using ladder stitch.

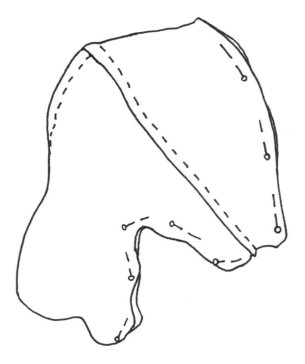

Figure 2

FINISH YOUR STAG

1. Decide where you would like your stag's eyes to be. I position them about 7.5cm (3in) apart and 6.5cm (2¾in) down from the antlers. Mark with tailor's chalk or an erasable fabric marker.

2. To make the eye dimples, I have a nifty method that means you don't end up with knots or ends. First cut a piece of thread about 80cm (32in) and fold it in half. Thread the two cut ends through the eye of the long needle, to make a big loop. Push the needle into one eye position and bring it out of the other eye – but don't pull it all the way; you want to leave a loop on the first side. (See Figure 3.)

3. Push the needle back in at the second eye, 0.2cm (⅛in) away from where it just came out, through to the first eye and through the loop. (See Figure 4.) Now pull the needle all the way, making the thread taut so that it dimples the eyes and gives the face some shape. When you're happy with the appearance, make a couple more stitches on each side, then finish by bringing the needle up some distance from the eye and snipping the thread neatly, so it disappears inside the the fabric and stuffing.

4. Now make a loop with the embroidery thread and stitch it to the marked position (given on the pattern) on the back head piece, so that you can hang your stag up for all to admire.

Figure 3

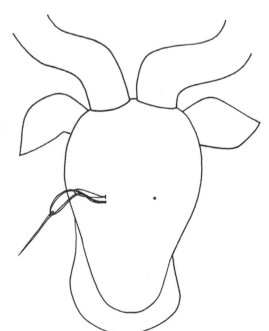

Figure 4

TIPS

Small prints work well for this project, although you could just as easily use a fine needle-cord fabric.

Experiment with bold, bright fabrics, as well as subtle, more classic designs.

free-machine embroidered cushion

I had been wanting to try my hand at free-machine embroidery for ages; I love how it takes away all the rules. You can just go where your needle takes you – even if you're using a template. If you've not tried it before, be warned that once you get the hang of it, free-machine embroidery is addictive. One of our talented tutors, Katy Berwick, came up with this gorgeous design. She's a mean free-machine embroiderer! You can see her work at etsy.com/shop/dropthedog

TIME

IF YOU HAVEN'T TRIED THIS SKILL BEFORE, I SUGGEST YOU PRACTISE FIRST TO BUILD YOUR CONFIDENCE. AS A RESULT, THIS IS PROBABLY QUITE A LENGTHY PROJECT. ONCE YOU'VE GOT USED TO THE TECHNIQUE, IT SHOULD TAKE ABOUT TWO OR THREE EVENINGS.

MATERIALS

CUSHION FABRIC:
1 X FRONT PIECE MEASURING 43CM X 43CM (17IN X 17IN), AND 2 X BACK PIECES MEASURING 43CM X 37CM (17IN X 15IN) – WE USED 100% LINEN

CONTRASTING AND CO-ORDINATING POLYESTER THREAD

TOOLS

SEWING MACHINE, INCLUDING DARNING FOOT

PATTERN PROVIDED AT THE BACK OF THE BOOK

FINE ERASABLE FABRIC PEN OR TAILOR'S CHALK PENCIL

15CM (6IN) DIAMETER EMBROIDERY HOOP

IRON

PINS

FABRIC SCISSORS

SET UP YOUR SEWING MACHINE AND TEMPLATE

1. First of all, set up your sewing machine. Following your machine's manual, lower the feed-dog (the teeth that are below the presser foot that draw the fabric through the machine). This will allow you to move the needle freely, as if you were drawing freehand with the needle.

2. Again, following your machine's manual, attach the darning foot. This will prevent the fabric from puckering and allows for more stability.

3. Set your machine to straight stitch and ensure the needle is positioned centrally. Don't worry about the stitch length; you will determine that by manually drawing the fabric through the machine. Thread your machine with the contrasting thread you want to use for the teacup.

4. Iron your fabric. Now trace the teacup outline onto your front piece of cushion fabric with the fine marker pen or chalk. Make sure the teacup is central and square on the fabric. Or you could trace directly onto the back of the paper template using tailor's chalk, then lay the template chalk-down on your fabric and trace the teacup with a pencil to transfer the chalk design to your fabric.

EMBROIDER THE TEACUP DESIGN

1. Attach the embroidery hoop to a central position of the teacup design. You need to attach the hoop in the opposite way to usual, so place the inner (smaller) hoop on top of the fabric and the outer (larger) hoop underneath. Secure and tighten the hoop. Pull the fabric through the hoop so that it is drum-tight. This is important! (See Figure 1.)

2. Raise the darning foot, and place the stretched fabric on the hoop underneath, ensuring the inner hoop is uppermost.

3. Lower the darning foot. Manually lower and raise the needle into the linen at your chosen startpoint using the fly-wheel; this should bring a loop of the lower (bobbin) thread up to the surface of the fabric. Carefully pull on the loop, so that you have two loose threads on the surface of the fabric – the top and bottom threads.

4. You're ready to sew! Turn the machine on and gently lower the pedal – make slow stitches at first. Rather than allowing the machine to pull the fabric through, you need to guide the fabric using the hoop, so that the needle follows the lines of the teacup. Try to keep the stitches even in length by moving the fabric/hoop at an even pace, but don't worry too much about following the template lines exactly: wiggly lines give the finished product an extra uniqueness and charm.

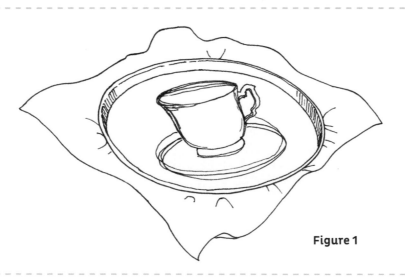

Figure 1

5. For the effect shown in the photograph, sew several lines of stitching over each other, tracing over the lines a few times. You don't need to secure your stitching at the start or end – just ensure it overlaps.

6. When you are close to the edge of the hoop, remove the fabric and reposition the hoop. You may need to do this several times until you have completed the whole design.

7. Once you've finished stitching, remove the fabric from the hoop and press it with a moderate iron.

MAKE THE CUSHION COVER

1. Set your machine back to standard sewing – replace the darning foot with a regular presser foot, change the thread to a coordinating colour, raise the feed-dogs and set the stitch length to medium.

2. Take the two smaller pieces of fabric. Fold over a 3cm (1in) hem down one of the 43cm (17in) sides on each piece, folding towards the back; press, and then fold over by another 3cm (1in). Pin and press, then stitch with a 2cm (¾in) seam allowance. (See Figure 2.)

3. Lay the embroidered fabric in front of you, right side up. Lay one smaller fabric piece on top, right side facing down. The raw edges should line up along the top, bottom and left-hand sides, and the neat hemmed edge should sit vertically, just right of centre. Pin in place.

4. Take the second smaller fabric piece and lie it on top with the right side facing down. The raw edges should line up along the top, bottom and right-hand sides this time, with the hemmed edge lying vertically left of centre. Pin in place.

5. Stitch all the way around the four edges of the cushion, leaving a 1.5cm (½in) seam allowance. (See Figure 3.)

6. Carefully trim the corners ensuring you don't cut too close to your stitching. Turn the cushion cover right side out.

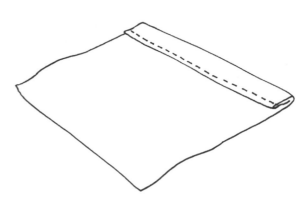

Figure 2

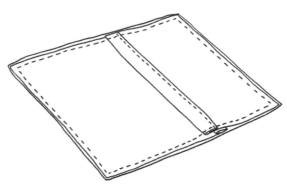

Figure 3

TIPS

Spend time experimenting with free-machine embroidery on scraps of fabric before you embark on this project. There's a definite knack to it that you'll need to get used to before you feel confident.

You can try out different coloured threads for the bobbin and spool (bottom and top) to create different effects. Don't stick rigidly to the lines of your template. Be free and spontaneous!

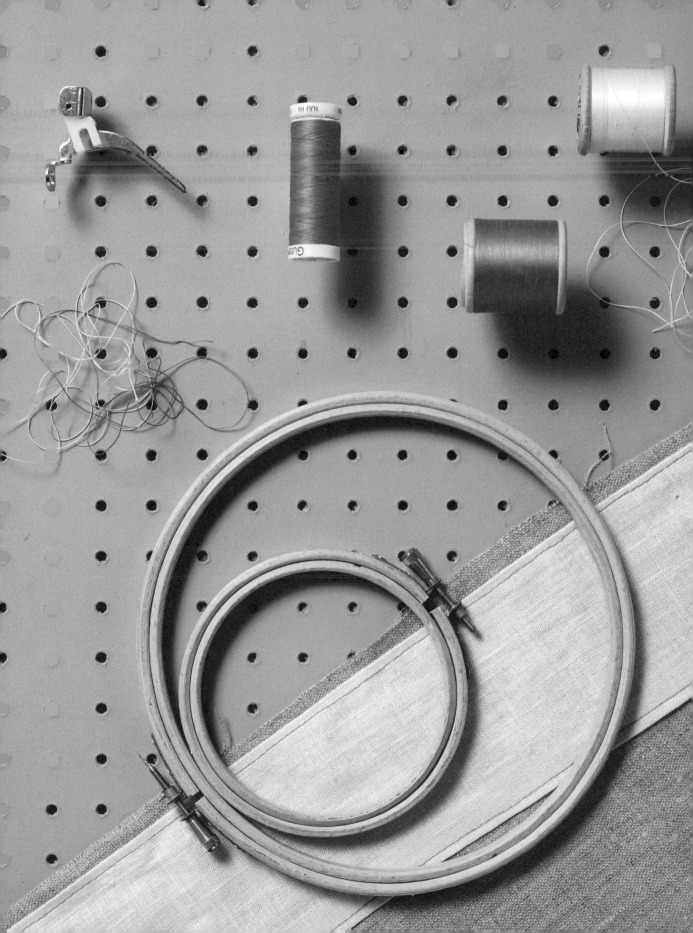

BUTTON Magnets

TIME

THIS SPEEDY PROJECT IS CERTAINLY DO-ABLE IN AN HOUR OR SO ONCE YOU'VE GATHERED THE MATERIALS YOU NEED.

Crafting is not just about creating labours of love – the beauty of making things for yourself is that the results are often far more impressive or delightful than you'd imagine for the amount of time they take. Button magnets are super-quick, but are an eye-catching touch in anyone's home. If you want to give them as a gift, try attaching them to cards rather like badges. Who wouldn't love them?

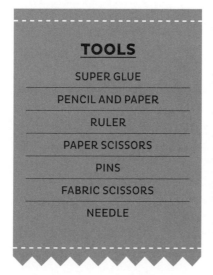

MATERIALS

A SELECTION OF REGULAR AND SELF-COVER FLAT-BACKED BUTTONS: LARGER THAN 1CM (¼IN) IN DIAMETER (SEE PAGE 155 FOR STOCKISTS)

CIRCULAR CERAMIC MAGNETS 0.95CM (¼IN) IN DIAMETER

SCRAPS OF LIGHT AND MEDIUM-WEIGHT COTTON, POLYESTER COTTON OR LINEN

CO-ORDINATING POLYESTER THREAD

TOOLS

SUPER GLUE

PENCIL AND PAPER

RULER

PAPER SCISSORS

PINS

FABRIC SCISSORS

NEEDLE

CONSTRUCT THE MAGNETS

1. Start with the regular buttons. Take the first button, put a blob of glue on the back and attach a magnet. Leave the glue to dry according to the glue instructions. Repeat for as many button magnets as you want to make.

2. For the self-cover buttons, first make a circular paper template that's 1cm (¼in) larger in circumference than the button you're using. Cut out the template, then pin it to a fabric scrap on a section of fabric that you'd like to feature on the magnet. Cut out the fabric around the template.

3. Take your needle and thread and knot the end. Sew a line of small running stitch (see page 148) around the circumference of the fabric, about 0.5cm (⅛in) in from the edge (see Figure 1).

4. Place the dish-shaped part of the button (the top) in the centre of the wrong side of the fabric circle, then pull your stitches to gather the fabric around it. Pull the thread tightly, and secure with a knot. (See Figure 2.)

5. Take the flat cover-button back and push down firmly over the back of the gathered fabric. (I sometimes use the end of a pencil for this.) Put a blob of glue on the back of the covered button, and stick on a magnet. Leave it to dry according to the glue instructions.

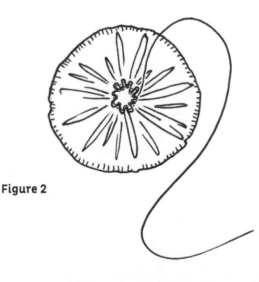

Figure 2

Figure 1

TIPS

Use strong ceramic magnets – the sort that are around 0.3cm (⅛in) thick. They need to be strong enough to hold your buttons on to the fridge or other metal surface, and attach through card.

Use only thin materials for this project. Thick fabric will make it impossible to secure the two parts of each self-cover button together.

PatchWORK Pouffe

TIME

THIS IS QUITE A TIME-CONSUMING PROJECT – THE STUFFING TAKES ALMOST AS LONG AS THE SEWING! YOU COULD PROBABLY DO IT IN A COUPLE OF EVENINGS AS LONG AS YOU DIDN'T HAVE TOO MANY DISTRACTIONS.

Once you've made this, you'll not want to sit on anything else! The lovely doughnut shape is so comfy, and you can mix and match the fabrics to suit your style. I've used a collection of new and old fabrics in sumptuous colours and textures.

TOOLS

PATTERN PIECE PROVIDED AT THE BACK OF THE BOOK

PINS

FABRIC SCISSORS

SEWING MACHINE

NEEDLE

UPHOLSTERY SKEWER, OR EXTRA-LONG NEEDLE

MATERIALS

OUTER FABRIC: ENOUGH FOR 6 X PIECES EACH MEASURING 60CM X 30CM (24IN X 12IN)

CO-ORDINATING POLYESTER THREAD

POLYESTER TOY STUFFING: 2KG (4½LB)

EXTRA-STRONG THREAD (SUCH AS LINEN OR BUTTONHOLE THREAD)

2 X LARGE BUTTONS, MINIMUM 3CM (1IN)DIAMETER, SUCH AS A LARGE WOODEN OR MOTHER-OF-PEARL BUTTONS

SEW THE PIECES TOGETHER

1. Lay the pattern template flat on your first fabric piece, then pin in place and cut out. Repeat for the remaining pieces, so you end up with six pieces of fabric all the same shape and size.

2. Decide in which order you would like to arrange the pieces (don't rush – you want it to look just right), then take two pieces that sit next to each other. Pin them together down one of the long curved edges, with right sides facing.

3. Set your machine to straight stitch (length around 2.5) and use a coordinating thread. Stitch down your pinned edge, with a 1.5cm (½in) seam allowance. Make sure you reverse at the beginning and end of your stitching, as it's essential the seams are strong. Switch your machine to zigzag, and sew another line of stitching within your 1.5cm (½in) seam allowance, close to (but not touching) your previous straight seam.

4. Take the next fabric in your scheme, and repeat step 3, joining the new piece to the two pieces already stiched together. Continue the process, gradually joining all of your pieces of fabric together until you have one (very) large piece with lots of seams and one open edge.

5. Match the two end pieces together, again with right sides facing, but ensure you leave a 25cm (10in) gap in your stitching. You might find the points (where all the fabrics meet in the middle at the top and bottom) are a little bit untidy, or there is a small gap. Don't worry, as you can fix this later on.

STUFF AND SHAPE THE POUFFE

1. Now turn your pouffe the right way out through the gap. We're going to half-stuff it first: just enough so that you can still feel your way around the inside. Take half your stuffing and push it right into the curves – all around the outside edge. Then squash the pouffe a little in the middle – like a doughnut. If you've over-stuffed at this point, it's trickier to do this step.

2. Thread your darning needle with at least 100cm (40in) of extra-strong thread. Pull all the way through so that you have a double thread, and tie a good strong knot in the end.

3. Push your needle through the bottom of the pouffe, just to the side of the centre point where all the fabrics meet. Thread it all the way through the middle (you will probably have to use two hands - one hand through the gap that you used to stuff), and wiggle the needle through until it comes out at the top, just to the side of where the fabrics meet. (See Figure 1.)

4. Thread the needle up through the back of one of your buttons, then down through the top. Then push the needle back through the pouffe, starting just to the side of the point where the fabrics meet, but this time on the opposite piece of fabric. Push the needle all the way through, the same way it came, so that it comes out of the bottom - again, just to the side of the point where the fabrics meet, but on the opposite piece of fabric.

5. When you've pushed your needle back through the bottom side, thread it through the other button in the same way you did at the top, and then you can pull your thread nice and tight - until your pouffe is as squished as you'd like it. The tighter you pull, the flatter and more doughnut-like it will be. There is still more stuffing to add to really pad it out, so make sure you leave space for that. Tie a knot behind the bottom button when you're happy with the look, and then finish stuffing the pouffe through the gap.

6. When it's nicely stuffed (remember it will compress over time), take your sewing needle and thread, and close the gap using ladder stitch (see page 149).

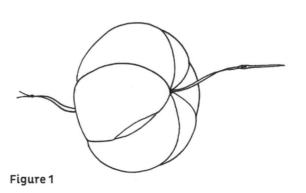

Figure 1

TIP

You can have as many fabric and colour combinations as you like; or this pouffe also looks good with just two different colours. Try to use fabrics of a similar weight, and make sure they're not too flimsy as they may take some wear and tear.

Tea Light Tins

TIME

HOW LONG THIS TAKES ENTIRELY DEPENDS UPON HOW COMPLICATED YOU WANT THE PATTERNS TO BE. I WOULD SET ASIDE A FULL AFTERNOON TO COMPLETE TWO OR THREE TINS. CHOOSE A DRY DAY SO YOU THAT CAN SPRAY-PAINT OUTDOORS.

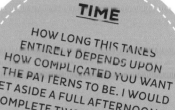

I love to decorate the trees in our garden during the summer, and I love tins – so for me this project is heavenly! These tea light holders look charming hanging from a tree in groups together as we enjoy the garden on a balmy evening.

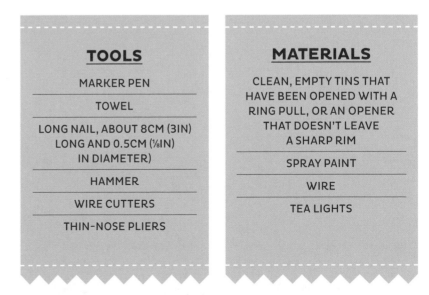

TOOLS

MARKER PEN

TOWEL

LONG NAIL, ABOUT 8CM (3IN) LONG AND 0.5CM (⅛IN) IN DIAMETER)

HAMMER

WIRE CUTTERS

THIN-NOSE PLIERS

MATERIALS

CLEAN, EMPTY TINS THAT HAVE BEEN OPENED WITH A RING PULL, OR AN OPENER THAT DOESN'T LEAVE A SHARP RIM

SPRAY PAINT

WIRE

TEA LIGHTS

MAKE YOUR HANGING LIGHTS

1. Mark dots on the tin where you'd like your holes to be using your pen. You could punch holes in a pattern (such as zigzags or curved lines), in shapes (hearts or stars, for example), or go for it freestyle. (See Figure 1.)

2. Put a towel on your work surface, to give some grip as you make the holes. Place the tin on its side on the towel and carefully hammer the nail into each mark, making a hole in the tin for each one. A heavier hammer will do this more easily. Don't underestimate how long this can take – reduce the number of holes if you become impatient to finish (I often do!).

3. Make two holes, on opposite sides of the top of the tin. These will provide holes for the hanging wire to thread through.

4. Spray-paint your tins according to the directions on the paint canister, trying to spray as evenly as possible. Do this step outside, to avoid fume inhalation and so that you don't make a mess indoors. Allow the paint to dry.

5. Cut a length of wire and thread each end through one of the holes you made at the top of the tin, bending the wire in place to secure it (see Figure 2). Put a tea light in each tin.

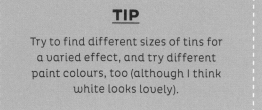

TIP

Try to find different sizes of tins for a varied effect, and try different paint colours, too (although I think white looks lovely).

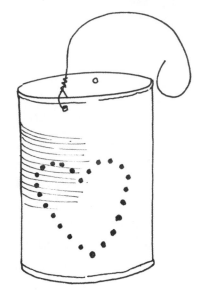

Figure 2

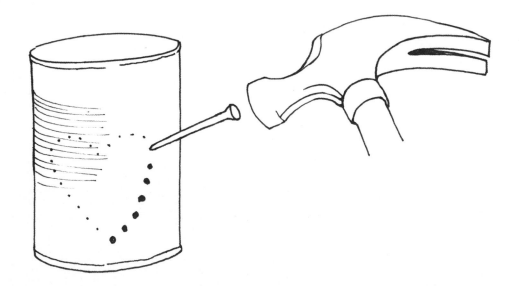

Figure 1

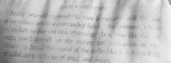

BOOK ENDS

The simple concept of a cuboid book end becomes a unique addition to your home with fabric panels printed using text from a favourite book. I used vintage sewing books for mine, but you could try anything you like, from a cherished novel to a childhood comic. These make brilliant doorstops, too!

TIME

THIS PROJECT CAN TAKE ONLY A COUPLE OF EVENINGS – ALTHOUGH I TOOK AGES DELIBERATING OVER WHAT TEXT TO USE.

TOOLS

RULER OR TAPE MEASURE

ERASABLE FABRIC PEN OR TAILOR'S CHALK

FABRIC SCISSORS

IRON

INKJET PRINTER

SEWING MACHINE

NEEDLE

MATERIALS

PIECE OF CALICO (UNBLEACHED COTTON FABRIC): 50CM X 110CM (20IN X 44IN)

A4-SIZED PIECE OF FREEZER PAPER (SEE PAGE 155 FOR STOCKISTS)

PRINTED MATERIAL, SUCH AS A VINTAGE BOOK

PIECE OF LINEN OR COTTON: 50CM X 110CM (20IN X 44IN)

CO-ORDINATING POLYESTER THREAD

POLYESTER TOY STUFFING

2 X 1KG/2LB BAGS OF RICE OR LENTILS

MAKE THE PRINTED FABRIC

1. From your calico, measure, mark and cut out one A4-sized piece (29.7cm x 21cm; 11¾in x 8¼in) and two rectangles each measuring 20cm x 15cm (8in x 6in).

2. Iron the freezer paper to the A4-sized piece of calico, with the shiny side towards the fabric and matt side uppermost. Use a medium setting, with the steam off, and make sure you don't iron the shiny side. The freezer paper sticks to and stiffens the fabric so that it will feed through your computer printer.

3. Place your printed matter on the printer. Feed the piece of paper-backed calico into your printer tray in the same way that you would normal paper, so that the fabric side will be printed on. Set the printer to make a copy.

4. Peel the freezer paper off the fabric and mark two rectangles 20cm x 15cm (8in x 6in) on the printed calico using a ruler or tape measure and erasable fabric pen or chalk. Cut out.

SEW UP THE BOOK ENDS

1. Cut the linen or cotton fabric into two strips, each measuring 75cm x 15cm (30in x 6in).

2. To attach the linen to the calico, with right sides facing, start at the midway point along the bottom of one printed calico piece, and pin one of the long sides of the linen around all four sides of the calico. Leave a 1cm (¼in) gap at the beginning and end. (See Figure 1.) Machine stitch in place with a 1cm (¼in) seam allowance.

3. Repeat this process with the other long side of the linen, joining it to an unprinted piece of calico, again with right sides together. Make sure the front and back pieces of calico are aligned. Stitch in place with a sewing machine. Clip all the corners to remove some of the bulk (see Figure 2).

4. Turn the book end right side out through the gap in the bottom. Press the seams to ensure you have a nice crisp cuboid shape.

5. Repeat steps 1 to 4 with the pieces of your second book end.

6. Fill the book ends completely with a combination of stuffing and rice or dried lentils, pushing the stuffing right into the corners and ensuring there's enough in there so that it doesn't sag.

7. Hand stitch the gaps together using ladder stitch (see page 149).

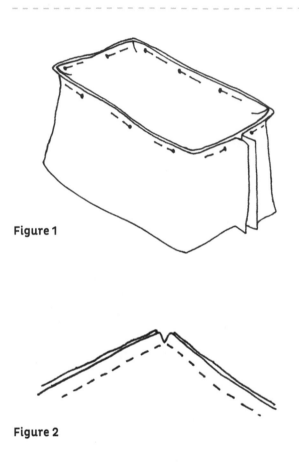

Figure 1

Figure 2

TIP

To give your bookends some grip, and help them hold up particularly heavy books, you could glue a square of oilcloth to the bottoms. This is particularly useful if you decide to use them as door-stops.

34   SIMPLE STITCHES

The third suggestion (59) is for ... ...ed cosy.
Seam your pieces together before ... ... you did
for the first cosy. Use emb... ... ...ate the
joins, and solid spots of ch... ... ... This
... was made in stripes of ... ...aterial
... ...rked in the same ... ... was of
... ...terial.

...tea cosy ... ...e motif
b... ... ...cles ... ... in the
book. White stitch... ... ...osy
and black on the wh... ... ... way,
but so that when th... ... ... black
came next to white and wh... ... ... lining
was in yellow. The fifth (61) has ... ... The last
(69) has strips of tape stitched down at even ... ... See that
the tape lies along the grain of the fabric. ... ...astened
down with a ... ...tch and p... ... ...e line of
stitching ...

The... ... ... and la... ... ...g ft.)
you will ... ...r decor... ... ...s cords
and ... ...e of ...

... ...ctive fo... ... ...you will
ne... ... ... silk for ... ...he belt.
car... ... ...ket. Cu... ... ...s of felt
th... ... ...nd 2" wide ... ...piece of
... ...slightly ... ...Make
your... ... ...od idea ... ...e paper
into ... ...y, leaf or ci... ... ...s one of
the... ... ...es it necessary ... ... trace it
acc... ... ...ions. Do no... ... leave a
space ... ...on and button... ... ...button-
hole end. F... ...locks better with the co... ... ...ded off.
Tack your design on to the felt by running ... ...e paper
and then tearing it off. Choose two or thr... ... ...and em-
b... ...he motif more thickly and firmly ... ...tch the

fifties frilly apron

Practical and pretty. This Fifties-inspired apron looks just as cute hanging in the kitchen as it does being worn.

TIME

ONCE YOU HAVE CUT OUT ALL THE FABRIC, YOU'LL BE ABLE TO COMPLETE THIS PROJECT IN TWO OR THREE AFTERNOONS.

MATERIALS

POCKET FABRIC: 40CM X 30CM (16IN X 12IN)

APRON FABRIC: 50CM X 110CM (20IN X 44IN)

WAISTBAND FABRIC: 20CM X 200CM (8IN X 79IN) – THERE CAN BE A JOIN IN THE MIDDLE

FRILL FABRIC: 20CM X 200CM (8IN X 79IN) – THERE CAN BE A JOIN IN THE MIDDLE

CO-ORDINATING POLYESTER THREAD

TOOLS

PATTERN PIECES PROVIDED AT THE BACK OF THE BOOK

PINS

FABRIC SCISSORS

IRON

NEEDLE

SEWING MACHINE

MAKE THE POCKETS

1. Cut out all the pattern pieces, then take the pocket fabric piece, and turn over the top straight edge towards the wrong side, by 1cm (¼in). Iron flat, then turn over another 2cm (¾in). Pin and iron, then machine stitch in place with a 1.5cm (½in) seam allowance.

2. Carefully fold over the curved edge of the pocket all the way round, towards the wrong side, by 1.5cm (½in). The trick to creating a great look is to keep the curves as neat as you can. To do this, make a few large tacked hand stitches around the curves, 0.5cm (⅛in) in from the edge (see Figure 1). Pull the hand stitching slightly to gather the pocket fabric and create a neatly curved edge. Pin in place and iron.

3. Position the pocket on the front of the apron – I like it off-centre, but it's entirely up to you. Pin in place, then machine top-stitch around the curved edges of the pocket, 0.5cm (⅛in) from the edge, to attach it to the apron fabric.

SEW THE APRON

1. Take the main apron fabric and fold each straight edge (the sides of the apron) towards the back by 1cm (¼in), and then again by another 1.5cm (½in). Pin and iron, then machine stitch in place 1cm from the edge.

2. To make the waistband, fold the waistband fabric 1cm (¼in) in towards the wrong side along all four edges. Iron to hold in place. Now fold the waistband in half, lengthways, with the wrong sides together. Iron in the crease.

3. Mark the centre of the waistband length with a pin. Also mark the centre of the top of the apron fabric. Open the folded waistband and slot the apron fabric halfway up inside the fold, making sure you match up the centre pins on the waistband and the apron. Pin in place.

4. With a 0.5cm (⅛in) seam allowance, machine stitch down the two short ends and along the bottom edge of the waistband, catching the apron fabric as you go. (See Figure 2.)

ADD THE FRILL

1. To make the frill, fold the frill fabric in half lengthways, right side out, and iron. Set your sewing machine to the longest straight stitch setting, and machine a line along the top raw edges of the fabric, 1cm (¼in) from the edge. Then sew another line of stitching 0.3cm (⅛in) in from the previous line. Note that you mustn't secure your stitching at either end.

2. Use the two lines of stitching to gather your frill. Carefully take the two ends of thread, grip them together, and ease the fabric through the threads to pull and gather it. (See Figure 3.) Repeat from the other end, until you have an evenly gathered length of fabric that measures 75cm (30in).

3. Position the frill upside down on the front of the apron, lining up the raw (gathered) edge of the frill with the bottom (raw) edge of the apron. Pin in place. Ease out 1cm (¼in) at each end of the frill, and fold over towards you (away from the apron front). Pin flat.

4. Set your machine back to medium stitch length (2-2.5) and stitch the frill to the apron along the bottom edge, 1cm (¼in) up from the raw edges.

5. Open out the frill and fold downwards. On the underside, pin the raw edge of the frill to the apron. Machine another line of stitching 0.5cm (⅛in) up from the previous line, catching the frill raw edges and the apron as you go.

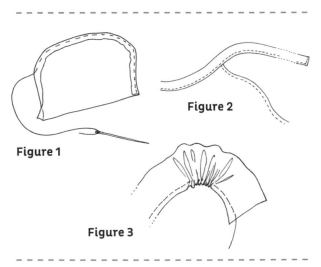

Figure 1

Figure 2

Figure 3

TIP

When you sew the frill, you may need to stop every now and then with the machine needle down, then lift the presser foot up to reposition the frills. Lower the foot again before continuing to sew.

Stitches & Tips

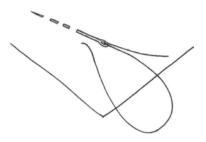

xxxxxxxxxxxxxxxxxxxxxxxxxxxxxxxxxxxxxxxxxxxxxxxxxxxxxxxxxx

If you are new to sewing, knitting, crochet or using a pattern, here are some of the basics to get you going, plus tips to make your crafting results even more professional-looking.

HAND STITCHING

HOW TO TIE AN INVISIBLE KNOT

1. Fold your thread in half to make a double thread, and pass the two cut ends through the needle. (The other end will be a loop.)

2. Starting on the right side of the fabric, push the needle through and then bring it back up again a tiny distance from where it went in, being careful not to pull the thread all the way through. You should have a loop of thread, through which you can push your needle. Pull the thread taut, and it will be secured without a bulky knot.

STITCH GUIDE

RUNNING STITCH

This can be used as a decorative stitch – it's nice and simple. Or it can be used to tack, or hand stitch pieces together that won't undergo too much stress. You can use double thread for more strength, if you like.

1. Thread a needle and knot the end. Bring the needle up through the back of the fabric.

2. Push the needle in and out of the fabric at regular intervals, following the line that you would like to stitch. You can vary the length of the stitches, and I don't push the needle in and out more than about three times at once, to ensure a nice even stitch.

3. Pull the needle through and repeat.

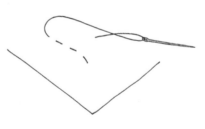

BACKSTITCH

This is stronger than running stitch, so used for seams and hems when more strength is required. It can be used as a decorative stitch.

1. Thread a needle and knot the end. Bring the needle up through the fabric.

2. Take one stitch through the fabric, then bring the needle up one full stitch length further along your stitching line.

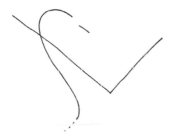

3. Put the needle into the point where your first stitch ended.

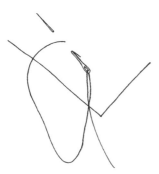

4. Bring the needle out a stitch length ahead of the previous finished stitch.

5. Keep working in this way to create a continuous line of stitching.

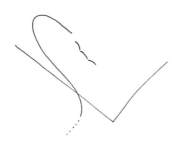

LADDER OR SLIP STITCH

One of my favourite stitches, I use this to join two pieces of fabric together.

1. Thread a needle and knot the end. Bring the needle up through the fabric on one side, where you'd like your stitching to begin.

2. At the same point on the other side of the gap to be closed, push the needle in and then out again, in the direction of stitching.

3. Keep working your way along the fabric, from one side to the other.

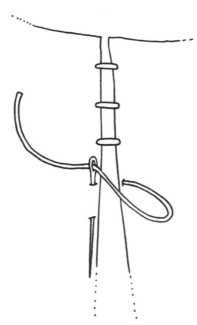

4. When you pull the thread taut, pull your stitching taut every few stitches. The stitches will be almost invisible, and nice and strong.

TIPS FOR SUCCESSFUL SEWING

PREPARING FABRIC

It is sensible to pre-wash all fabric before you start any sewing project. This is to avoid shrinkage after you've made your item, as most fabrics do shrink in the wash. Iron all pieces, too.

IRONING AS YOU SEW

Usually I'm not very friendly with my iron. However, it is an indispensable tool when sewing. Ironing your seams as you go can make the difference between a project that looks OK, and a project that looks really professional.

PINS

I always use glass-headed pins for sewing – mainly because, unlike plastic-headed pins, they don't melt under the iron. They also look pretty and are easier to spot than metal-headed pins if you drop them.

Some people swear by pinning perpendicular to their stitching and sewing over the pins, but I am an advocate of pinning in the same direction as the line of stitching and removing the pins as you go. It's important that the pinheads are facing you, to make removing them easier.

TACKING

Tacking fabric in place with hand stitches means you don't need to manoeuvre your sewing machine around pins. You can use cheap tacking thread in a colour that stands out against your fabric and make reasonably large stitches (around 2cm/¾in long). Simply remove the tacking stitches once you've machined over them.

If I'm honest, I rarely tack these days. However, if you're making something that is either extremely important, that uses very fine fabrics, or has lots of fiddly corners, it is wise to tack.

CLIPPING CORNERS

This removes bulky fabric and means your finished piece will look far neater. I like to use a sharp pair of embroidery scissors, since they're nice and small. When you've sewn the corner, with the fabric still inside out, snip off the tip of the corner diagonally, making sure you leave at least 0.3cm (⅛in) between your cut and the line of stitching, to ensure it doesn't fray. Then turn the fabric right side out and press flat.

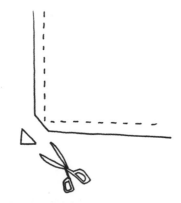

CLIPPING CURVES

This also removes bulk, to ensure a smoother curve. When you've sewn the curve, make small V-shaped snips around it – I use small embroidery scissors – making sure you leave at least 0.3cm (⅛in) between the tip of your cut and the line of stitching. Turn the fabric right side out and press flat.

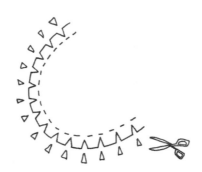

USING SEWING PATTERNS

GRAIN

Woven fabrics are made up of threads that run horizontally and vertically. The direction that the threads run is called the 'grain' of the fabric. If you try to stretch the fabric in the direction that the threads run, you'll notice there isn't really any give. On many patterns, you will see a line with an arrow at either end. It's important that this line follows the direction of the grain - to ensure the fabric sits straight on your finished piece. For example, if you were to make a skirt and the grain wasn't aligned, you'd find the skirt just wouldn't sit correctly, and would keep twisting round. Not a good look!

BIAS

The bias of a woven fabric runs diagonal to the grain. If you try and stretch the fabric on the bias, you'll notice it has quite a lot of stretch to it. Fabric cut on the bias hangs in a much softer way, due to the stretch. Note that this doesn't apply to knitted (jersey) fabrics.

SELVEDGE

This is the finished edge of a whole width of woven fabric. Often it has a white unprinted strip. The selvages are useful for double-checking the grain of the fabric.

NOTCHES

You'll notice little triangles at the edge of pattern pieces. Where you see them, it's important that you cut the notches into your fabric, too – they are there to ensure you match pattern pieces accurately.

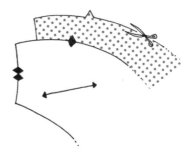

SEAM ALLOWANCE

The distance between your stitching and the edge of the fabric. For dressmaking, this tends to be 1.5cm (½in). The plate below your sewing machine's presser foot should have markings that will help you measure the seam allowance.

USING A SEWING MACHINE

STARTING AND FINISHING YOUR STITCHING

It is important that your stitching is secured, to ensure it doesn't come undone. The quickest and sturdiest way of doing this is to make a few reverse stitches.

AT THE START

1. I think it's good practice to do the very first stitch of any line manually. That way, you have complete control over where your stitching begins and the speed at which you're sewing. Turn the balance wheel towards you until the needle has completed one stitch. (Avoid turning the wheel away, as it can knot the threads.)

2. Lower your foot on the pedal and sew three to four stitches. Then hold down the reverse lever (check your manual for its whereabouts) and make three to four stitches backwards, sewing over your previous stitching.

3. Now you're good to stitch, knowing that your sewing is secured nice and tightly.

AT THE END

1. When you've finished your stitching, hold the reverse lever down and make three to four stitches back over your work.

2. Now you can raise the presser foot and pull out your fabric, trimming the thread close to your stitches.

WITH FINE FABRICS

1. Rather than reversing, leave a long tail at the start of stitching. Turn your fabric so the wrong side is facing upwards.

2. Hold the thread at the end of the stitching and give it a pull – this will bring a loop of thread.

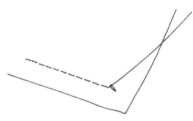

3. Pull this loop with a pin.

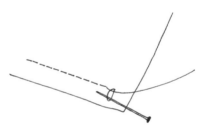

4. This will pull the upper thread through to the back. Then knot the two threads together securely.

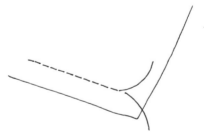

SEWING MACHINE MAINTENANCE

NEEDLE

If your machine stitching starts missing the odd stitch, it could mean your needle is blunt and needs changing.

OIL

Many machines come with a little bottle of oil. If not, they're easy enough to come by in sewing machine retailers. It's worth oiling monthly if you use your machine regularly. If it starts to sound less happy and smooth, brush all the collected dust from the bobbin area and give it a good oil. Make sure you do a piece of test sewing straight afterwards, in case some of the oil transfers.

KNITTING

The basic stitches and how they are abbreviated in knitting patterns.

CASTING ON (CAST ON OR CO)

1. Make a slip knot in the end of the yarn. Place the knot on a knitting needle and pull tight.

2. Hold the needle with the slip knot in your left hand. With the other needle in your right hand, insert the right needle into the stitch on the left-hand needle. Take the yarn still connected to the ball and wrap it once under and around the right-hand needle.

3. Pull the looped yarn back through using the point of the right needle, to make a stitch. Slip the stitch onto the left-hand needle.

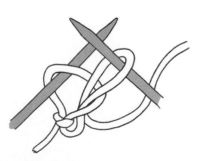

4. Repeat steps 2–3 until you have reached your desired total number of stitches, but for all following stitches, instead of inserting the needle into the left-hand stitch, insert it in between the previous two stitches.

KNIT STITCH (OR K)

1. Hold your needles so that the stitches are on your left needle, the other needle is in your right hand, and the yarn is at the back. Insert the right needle into the first stitch on your left needle and hold it behind the left needle at right angles. Wind the yarn under and around the right-hand needle.

2. Pull the looped yarn back through the stitch towards you, using the tip of the right-hand needle.

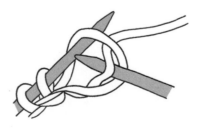

3. Pull the new stitch (on your right-hand needle) off the left-hand needle.

4. Repeat steps 1–3 for all the stitches, until you have reached the end of the row. Now turn the knitting round and hold the full needle in your left hand, ready for the next row.

PURL (OR P)

1. Hold your needles so that the stitches are on your left needle, the other needle is in your right hand, and the yarn is at the front. Insert the right needle into the front of the first stitch from right to left. Wind the yarn over and around the right hand needle.

2. Pull the looped yarn back through the stitch using the tip of the right needle, and push the old stitch towards the needle tip.

3. Slide the new stitch (on your right-hand needle) off the left-hand needle.

4. Repeat steps 1–3 for all the stitches, until you have reached the end of the row. Now turn the knitting round and hold the full needle in your left hand, ready for the next row.

CASTING OFF (CAST OFF OR BIND OFF)

1. This gives a neat edge when you finish. Start the row with two knit stitches. Then with the yarn at the back, push the left-hand needle into the right-hand stitch on the right-hand needle.

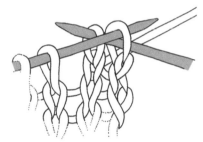

2. Using the tip of your left-hand needle, pull the loop of the first stitch on the right-hand needle over the top of the second one, as shown – so that only the second stitch remains on the right hand needle.

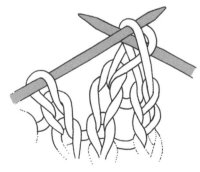

3. Knit another stitch in the usual way, then repeat step 2 (see Figure 3). Carry on in this way until you reach the end of the row, when you should end up with one stitch on the right-hand needle.

4. Cut your yarn leaving a 20cm (8in) tail – unless a longer tail is specified. Slip the tail of yarn through the final stitch on your needle, and pull it to tighten the loop.

5. To neaten at the end, thread the yarn onto a darning needle and weave it through a few of the stitches, before snipping off the end.

CROCHET

The basic stitches and how they are abbreviated in crochet patterns.

MAKING A CHAIN (CH)

1. Make a slip knot in the end of your yarn, and thread it onto your crochet hook.

2. Hold the hook in the same way you would a pen.

3. Wind the long end of yarn around the fingers of your other hand as shown, looping it around your little finger to control the tension in the yarn.

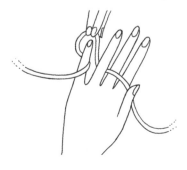

4. Now wind the yarn around the hook, bringing it towards you.

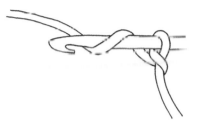

5. Bring the new loop on your hook back through the original (slip) loop: one chain stitch complete! You should have one loop on the hook.

6. Continue to make more loops – chain stitches – in the same way.

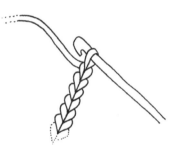

DOUBLE CROCHET (DC)

1. You need to add an extra chain stitch at the beginning of every new row of double crochet, to act as a turning chain; it means you can bring the hook up at the right height for the new row.

2. For the first row, insert the hook through the front of the third stitch away from the hook, from front to back.

3. Wind the yarn around the hook, bringing it towards you.

4. Bring the loop back through the chain stitch.

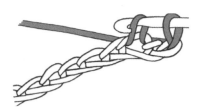

5. Wind the yarn around the hook and bring it back through both loops that are already on the hook, so that you have one new loop on your hook: one double crochet stitch has now been made.

6. Insert the hook into the next chain stitch and repeat the process to the end of the row.

7. For the second and all consecutive rows, make one chain stitch to bring the hook up to the right height for your new row. Then insert the hook into the second double chain stitch of the previous row and create a double crochet stitch. Continue to the end, inserting the hook into every double crochet stitch and creating a new one.

FASTENING OFF

1. When you've finished your crochet, you need to fasten off neatly. You should have one stitch left on your hook. Wrap the yarn around your hook, and then bring it back through the loop. Trim the end of yarn to about 30cm (12in), and then pull the end all the way through the loop.

2. Remove the hook, and pull the yarn tightly through the loop to secure it.

JOINING SEAMS

I think this is the best way to join seams in a neat and flat fashion. You'll need a darning needle threaded with the same yarn as your work.

1. Place the two edges of crochet in front of you, with right sides facing up, then match up the stitches of each piece, row to row.

2. Starting on one side, bring the needle up through the top of the first stitch. Then push it back down through the bottom of the stitch on the same side.

3. Now take your yarn over to the other side, and repeat the process – working your way down. Secure your yarn.

STOCKISTS

Pendant bases
themakeryonline.co.uk
kernowcraft.com
etsy.com

Spray fixative or sealer
michaels.com
quickdrawsupplies.com

Mod Podge
themakeryonline.co.uk
calicocrafts.co.uk
michaels.com

Gütermann HT2 fabric glue
themakeryonline.co.uk
u-handbag.com

Purse clasps
themakeryonline.co.uk
u-handbag.com

Debbie Bliss yarn
woolbath.co.uk
texere-yarns.co.uk
knittingfever.com

Erika Knight yarn
woolbath.co.uk
bluewaterfibers.com
loopknitlounge.com

Shrink plastic
themakeryonline.co.uk
wizardtoys.com

Stazon ink pads
themakeryonline.co.uk
stampaddictsshop.co.uk
michaels.com

Jewellery findings
beadsunlimited.co.uk
michaels.com

Wadding and batting
cottonpatch.net
joann.com

Flex-frames
themakeryonline.co.uk
u-handbag.com

Erasable fabric pens
quiltdirect.co.uk
habbyworld.co.uk

Small circular mirrors
hobbycraft.co.uk
dickblick.com

Wool felt
bloomingfelt.co.uk

Iron-on vinyl and oil cloth
themakeryonline.co.uk
createforless.com

Interfacing
habbyworld.co.uk
joann.com

Cord elastic
joann.com
hobbycraft.co.uk

Wooden toggles
themakeryonline.co.uk
www.joann.com

Split ring keyring findings
themakeryonline.co.uk
shop.hobbylobby.com

Japanese washi tape
themakeryonline.co.uk
outotape.com

Wooden cotton reels
themakeryonline.co.uk

Lino-cutting tools
greatart.co.uk
shop.hobbylobby.com

Baker's twine
themakeryonline.co.uk
whiskergraphics.com

Felt hearts and balls
bloomingfelt.com

Clock mechanisms
hobbycraft.co.uk
shop.hobbylobby.com

Embroidery hoops
sewandso.co.uk
michaels.com

Toy stuffing
fredaldous.co.uk
joann.com

Vintage comics
americandreamcomics.co.uk

Self-cover buttons
themakeryonline.co.uk
etsy.com

Circular magnets
cuddlybuddly.com
shop.hobbylobby.com

Mother-of-pearl buttons
themakeryonline.co.uk
joann.com

Freezer paper
bookdepository.co.uk
walmart.com

INDEX

Acknowledgements

Thank you to Denise Bates and all at Octopus Publishing Group for your support in making this book possible.

Marc Wilson, Martha Gavin, Aliki Kirmitsi and Ania Wawrzkowicz, and Luke Wright and Ross Imms at A-Side Studio; thank you all for being so wonderfully creative and bringing our vision alive so beautifully.

Also to Judy Barratt, Jenni Moore, Vick Millar and Eirlys Penn for their help in editing, checking and refining the text.

Huge thanks to Kate and Darren (owners of the gorgeous valeviewbath.co.uk), and to Michaela Eyston and family and Vick Millar and family for allowing us to take over their houses for rather longer than they probably imagined for the photographs in this book.

Thank you to the very talented Sara Huntington, Katy Berwick and Jessica Biscoe for their time and skill in designing their projects.

A massive thank you to Laura at Wool for her generosity and general loveliness. You're too kind!

Thank you to Caroline Garland and Ollie Langdon for being so gorgeous and bringing the pages alive. And to Bridie Roman, and Anna Hext and Alice Woolliscroft for your help preparing and on shoot days.

Colossal thanks to our Sarah Cunniffe for her wonderful smiles and support. And to her mum for making her so wonderful. And thank you to Cerys Gasson and all our other wonderful staff at The Makery, who have kept things going whilst I've been busy Making.

Of course, thank you to Caroline Harris and Clive Wilson for asking us in the first place and keeping me going.

And finally thank you most of all to Nigel for everything you do, and embracing our Makery way so wholeheartedly. And my mum, her mum and I suspect her mum too; for passing on the Making gene and encouraging me from such a young age.

DISCARD